PADDLE
ROUTES
OF THE INLAND NORTHWEST

PADDLE ROUTES

OF THE INLAND NORTHWEST

**50 FLATWATER AND
WHITEWATER
TRIPS FOR
CANOE & KAYAK**

RICH LANDERS
DAN HANSEN

THE
MOUNTAINEERS

This book is dedicated to our families,
and to others who seek wild times on rivers.

 Published by
The Mountaineers
1001 SW Klickitat Way, Suite 201
Seattle, WA 98134

First printing 1998, second printing 1999

Published simultaneously in Great Britain by Cordee, 3a DeMontfort Street, Leicester, England, LE1 7HD

Manufactured in the United States of America

Edited by Uma Kukathas
Maps by Warren Huskey
Cover design by Amy Peppler Adams, designlab—Seattle
Book design by Alice C. Merrill
Layout by Michelle Taverniti

Cover photograph: *Jean and Kevin Dragon on Lower Palouse River,* by Rich Landers
Frontispiece: *Canoeist paddles into basin below Palouse Falls,* by Rich Landers

Library of Congress Cataloging-in-Publication Data
Landers, Rich, 1953–
    Paddle routes of the Inland Northwest : 50 flatwater and whitewater trips for canoe and kayak / Rich Landers, Dan Hansen.
        p.   cm.
    Includes index.
    ISBN 0-89886-556-5
    1. Canoes and canoeing—Northwest, Pacific—Guidebooks.
2. Kayaking—Northwest, Pacific—Guidebooks. 3. Canoes and canoeing—British Columbia—Guidebooks. 4. Kayaking—British Columbia—Guidebooks. 5. Northwest, Pacific—Guidebooks. 6. British Columbia—Guidebooks. I. Hansen, Dan. II. Title.
    GV776.N76L36 1998
    917.9504'43—dc21   97-45681
                                                                                      CIP

CONTENTS

BRITISH COLUMBIA

IDAHO

OREGON

MONTANA

APPENDICES

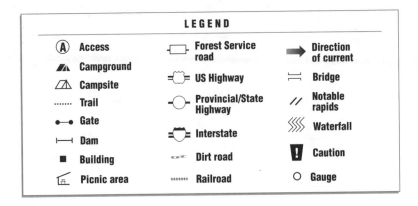

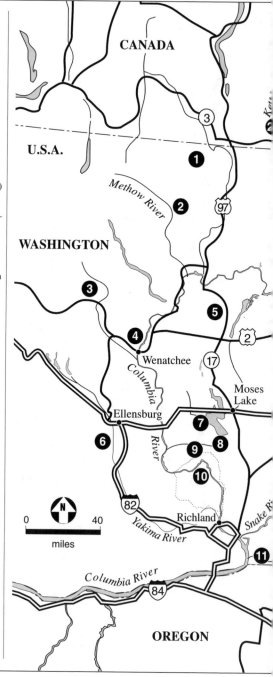

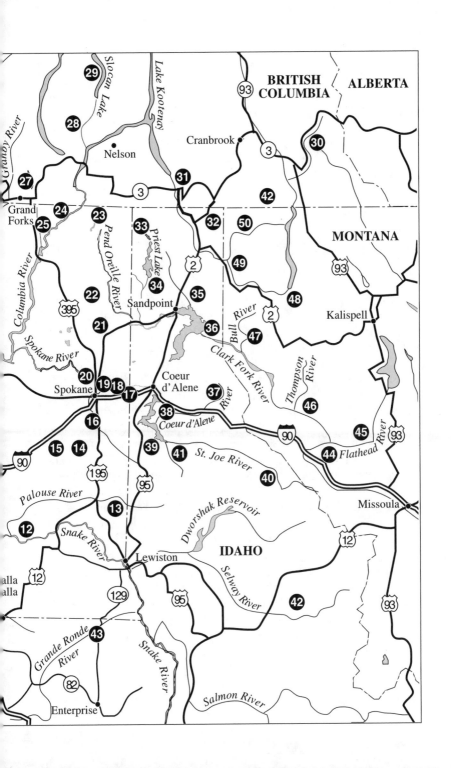

PREFACE

Let's be honest up front. Two personalities in close proximity spell a potential for trouble. Ask any couple in a canoe or other contraption that forces a pair of weary bodies to work as one machine. Some of these engines purr. Some of them smoke.

Fights are common among harnessed sled-dog teams. Why should we expect stressless performance in the shackles of a tandem canoe? Soloists have no one to blame for headwinds or a scary encounter with Deadman Rapids. Tandem travelers have a handy human scapegoat. Often, the paddler in the stern has nothing better to do than scrutinize every draw, pry, daydream, and nose wipe the bow paddler makes. Spokane Canoe & Kayak Club instructors routinely separate couples in entry-level paddling clinics to prevent bloodshed.

Some couples thrive in close proximity. Others sink into conflicts arising from classic points of contention, such as which way is left. The bickering usually comes to a head when the new $1,000 canoe smacks against the only protruding rock in a mile of river.

Once *both* paddlers have instruction, harmony is easier to achieve.

Here's the bottom line. We love canoeing, and our marriages have survived it. Our kids haven't run away from home. For every point of contention there have been dozens of cherished moments: The loon's call during a full-moon paddle on a glassy lake. Eight months pregnant and the paddle trip with a thousand pit stops. The bluff charge of a cow moose. Oldest daughter landing her first trout with everyone leaning toward the same side of the canoe. That first snappy eddy turn in a stiff current. Skinny dipping at a backcountry camp. The mallard hen leading her fuzzy yellow ducklings past the bow. Plopping the kids in their first sea kayaks and watching them paddle off alone.

Paddling is an enormously pleasurable and versatile sport, from the rush of whitewater to the serenity of flatwater. You can do it when you are young and free, or while parenting the kids. Seniors who still want to camp and explore find particular pleasure in having a boat to carry the packs.

A canoe or kayak can take you to the best places and memories in life, so long as you don't go overboard.

Peek-a-boo on the St. Maries River (Rich Landers photo)

ACKNOWLEDGMENTS

Our thanks to the members of the Spokane Canoe & Kayak Club, particularly those who over the years provided trip reports for the club newsletter. Many of those reports served as the early research for trips in this book. Some of the members who provided additional assistance include Julie Titone, Brian Burns, Dick Easterly, Larry Wood, Vic and Robbi Castleberry, Tom Smith, David White, John and Megan Roland, and Ron and Jane McDonald.

Special thanks to Tim McWilliams and Al Randall for sharing their superb knowledge of western Montana rivers, and to Jean and Kevin Dragon, who were always ready to explore new waters.

Brad and Debbie Summers, Doris Albert, Gerhardt Glaas, Jim Gillman, Bill Demchuk, and Gordon Silverthorne were more than helpful in British Columbia. Frem Nielsen skillfully piloted his Cessna when the necessary route was by air instead of water. The staff at Northwest Map and Travel Service in Spokane were invaluable resources.

Thanks to Ray and Nancy Hansen, Keith Hansen, Steve Thompson, Bart Rayniak, Jack Nisbet, Everett Combs, Dale Bartholomew, Gary Burgess, Cheryl and Brittney Hartshorn, Kent and Julia Larsen, and on-call baby-sitters Claudia Schroder and Ralph and Mary Lou West.

Richard and Kathy Spencer, Miller Brown, Alita Humphrey, Josie Merithew, Dick Lee, Bob Snider, Dick Roberts, and Rick Gren offered shuttles and advice near their home waters. Steve Weinberger and Mac McCandless get a pat on the back for keeping us on their Christmas card list even though the holiday was only a month after the unplanned swim in the Elk River.

Ainsworth Paddles, Sawyer Paddles and Oars, Lotus Designs, and Dagger Canoes assisted with products that aided in the research for this book.

And thanks to our families, whose patience, support, and willingness to get wet made this book possible.

INTRODUCTION

WHY THIS BOOK? THE WATERS NEED YOU

Whitewater isn't everything, but you'd never know it by scanning the shelves of bookstores throughout the West. Whitewater is where the action is: the best photos, the biggest rush. This is where most of the guidebook effort has been.

Unfortunately, whitewater doesn't appeal to the masses of potential paddlers, nor does it describe the majority of paddling routes. The roar of rapids enthuses experienced boaters while it intimidates paddlers who are still improving their skills. Whitewater can be downright terrifying to parents with children.

This book fills a niche that has been sorely neglected in the Inland Northwest. The trips section concentrates on waters generally within the limits of beginning or intermediate paddlers. Experienced paddlers regularly ply these waters, too.

Encouraging new paddlers is the immediate reason for this book. The larger motivation is for the future.

The Call for Conservation

Paddlers who develop an intimacy with a lake or river become its best friends. They tend to learn about a water's past and present. Ultimately, they become influential in its future.

Some Northwest rivers are flooded with more issues than water. Did you know, for instance, that at one point near Twin Falls, Idaho, the mighty Snake River is sucked dry for irrigation? A century of mining has left portions of the Coeur d'Alene River with toxic levels of heavy metals that kill unknown numbers of migrating tundra swans and other waterfowl each year. There's a chance that private development could permanently block access to small but intriguing Horseshoe Lake in Washington's Spokane County.

Endangered species protection, pollution discharges, hydropower dams, and human settlement on and off the shorelines are just a sampling of the myriad issues that must be addressed for Western waters including those described in this book.

Hydropower relicensing is a sleeper in the movement to preserve rivers. Utility companies across the country were authorized to build dams decades ago with licenses that expired after fifty years. In 1993, about 260 licenses affecting 105 rivers came up for renewal. Local conservationists who rose to the cause influenced the criteria for relicensing to improve flows for fish and recreation.

Another 550 dam licenses expire through the year 2010. This round of relicensing may be the last chance for a generation to influence the management of key rivers.

Conservation begins with individuals who get to know a stretch of water, who learn to enter it gently, float its length, take out with care, and encourage others to do the same. Paddlers, rafters, and anglers tend to know rivers better than casual river visitors. That's why there's a clear connection between conservation and recreation.

Gains in river conservation often come slowly, lake by lake, river by river, rapid by rapid. Efforts to protect or restore a river can range from the subtle fencing of an access area to the dramatic removal of a dam.

When the city of Spokane proposed raising the level of Upriver Dam in the early 1990s, only a few paddlers and anglers protested to the Federal Energy Resource Commission. For roughly $115,000 of additional energy production a year, the city would inundate more wildlife habitat and destroy a captivating riffle where paddlers play and trout spawn. The casual observer may see this as insignificant. Those who are intimate with the river have a different perspective.

The Spokane River is 111 miles long from its source at Lake Coeur d'Alene to its confluence with the Columbia River. Less than 36 miles—20 percent—of the river remain free flowing. The remaining rapids can be counted on two hands. Time has come to fight for every remaining riffle.

Combining forces, conservationists can demand mitigation for development that degrades rivers. They can demand wetland restoration, fish ladders, and screens on diversion intakes. They can call for toning down flow fluctuations that are a nightmare for boaters and fish alike.

River otter, found in most major undammed rivers in the Inland Northwest (Rich Landers photo)

What You Can Do

Accompany a hunting or fishing group, conservation organization, or paddling club and help plant shoreline habitat, clean up the stream channel, or fence cattle off the fragile banks. Public land agencies are more and more receptive to citizen work parties. Be willing to meet with government officials and write letters. First-hand testimony about the importance of natural river systems is influential in government decisions, but often lacking.

Of course, a paddler's lifestyle should reflect allegiance to the river, too. Use water and electricity judiciously. Take care in what you pour down drains and sewers. Petroleum products and toxic chemicals should go to disposal facilities, not in your river.

Join conservation groups, such as those listed in Appendix F. A chorus of unified voices speaks louder than scattered solos. Also, know your allies. Anglers and paddlers have much in common. So do rafters and canoeists, birdwatchers and kayakers, hunters and campers.

In an age of divisiveness, rivers connect us all.

HOW TO USE THIS GUIDEBOOK

Each river or lake discussed in this book warrants its own guidebook to cover the history, flora, fauna, conservation issues, and details about the route. This book is designed to give only an overview. Some details are left out to leave something for you to discover on your own. Other specifics are avoided because rivers and lakes change dramatically with different flows and levels. The land around these waters, too, is subject to change.

This book describes basic details paddlers should know to complete a specific tour, as well as information useful in further exploration. Some terms used in the text may be unfamiliar to those new to the sport. For instance, to avoid confusion when giving directions on a stream, "river-right" means to the right shore as you face downstream. See the glossary of paddling terms in Appendix G.

The following detailed summary is included at the beginning of each trip.

Distance: Length of the paddling route in miles.

Paddling time: Conservative gauge of the time one must spend on the water to complete the trip; references to several days or "overnight" identify trips suitable for camping.

Season: Months the waters generally are free of ice or have sufficient water for paddling. Be aware that runoff events can make rivers unsafe for paddlers for short periods during the floating season.

Shuttle: Distance one must drive one-way between the put-in and take-out, plus guides to road conditions.

Rating: Subjective evaluation to give paddlers a quick sense of the skills required. This is the most difficult detail to provide, because river ratings can change week to week. High flows can be easy or scary, depending on your skill level. The ratings used are based on the International Scale of River Difficulty outlined in the Safety Code of the American Whitewater Affiliation. The code is described in more detail later in this introduction.

Hazards: Notable features that could spell trouble for paddlers. Before launching, give careful consideration to the water conditions and your skill level (plus the experience of other boaters in your party), combined with the possibility of encountering noted hazards such as logjams and wind.

Information: Who to contact for up-to-date information on water conditions or the area involved in the specific trip. See Appendix B for telephone numbers for the agencies or businesses noted here.

Maps: Specific United States Geological Survey (USGS) topographical maps that cover the trip. Canada maps are prepared by the federal Department of Energy, Mines, and Resources (EMR). Maps useful in showing access roads or public land also are listed.

The opening paragraphs of each trip description provide an overview of the nature and difficulty of the journey, the character of the landscape, and the flora and fauna one might encounter.

The section on "Access" provides detailed driving directions to the put-in and take-out.

Each trip description or "Paddle Route" begins, where possible, with the following river and water flow information. (Note that such facts are not available for all trips described in this book. Paddlers should consult the agencies listed under "Information" at the beginning of each trip to see if any details are available. Again, telephone numbers for the agencies are given in Appendix B.)

Flow information: Sources for up-to-date readings on river flows. Lake level information is substituted when applicable. All flows in this book are listed in cubic feet per second (cfs), even though Canadian gauges record flows in cubic meters per second. To convert Canadian readings to cfs, multiply the metric flow by 35.

River gauge: Official number for the station that measures flows closest to the trip described. This number is especially helpful for Internet users seeking information on the World Wide Web.

Historic flows: General guide to how much water flows down a river based on years of data collected at gauging stations. "Average" is the mean flow for an entire year, "maximum" the highest recorded flow to the date of this book's publication, "minimum" the lowest recorded flow.

SAFETY CONSIDERATIONS

With proper instruction and common sense, paddling is a safe sport for people of all ages. Like any outdoor activity, it is hazardous for the ill-prepared or foolhardy.

Wear the proper clothing and carry safety equipment. Practice the J-stroke, the pry, the draw, and other basic strokes. Learn to ferry, with both a forward stroke and a back stroke, so you can avoid hazards. Team up with at least one other canoe on moving water, and agree to avoid water that makes the weakest paddler feel uncomfortable. The leader of any trip should go down a stream first to check the channel. A boat with a strong paddler or paddlers should be designated as the sweep to be sure everyone gets downstream safely. Scout ahead on unfamiliar stretches of river, and portage or line the boat around any downed trees or whitewater that is beyond your ability.

Boaters also should become familiar with local waterway laws.

Be realistic about your abilities. The Sullivan Rapids of the Spokane River is not the place to learn basic paddle strokes, nor is spring runoff the time to take your first trip into whitewater. Respect for water is the key to safety.

Finally, boating and booze don't mix. Alcohol affects balance, impairs judgment, and increases the effects of the cold. The American Canoe Association reports that more than half of all boating accidents and drownings involve people who have been drinking. Play it safe; save any spirits for camp.

Gauging a River

River flows are critical to paddlers. High flows generally mean cold, fast water that washes out eddies, generates turbulence, and creates difficulty in getting to shore should a boat capsize. Low flows can leave a canoe bouncing on rocks instead of waves. High flows might create play areas on some rivers, but wash out attractive rapids on others. Many paddlers prefer the more technical challenge of negotiating river obstacles when river flows are down.

When possible, this book offers subjective information on prime flow rates for paddlers. Sources of stream flow information are listed with trip descriptions. Also listed is the gauge number, which speeds the research, especially for paddlers with Internet access. Most navigable rivers have gauges that monitor flows in cubic feet per second, although the information often is not immediately accessible. Smaller streams may have gauges that are not operating because of damage or funding shortages.

World Wide Web sites with information on stream flows include *http://www.idaho.wr.usgs.gov/* for Idaho, *http://www.dmthln.cr.usgs.gov/* for Montana, *http://nimbo.wrh.noaa.gov/Portland* for Oregon, and *http://www.dwatcm.wr.usgs.gov/* for Washington. Information useful to paddlers generally is under "current hydrological data" and "realtime water resources." The National Weather Service also monitors stream flows in some areas.

Flows are recorded on most major rivers in Canada, but the government has been slow to make the information public. For progress reports, contact Water Survey Canada, Suite 120, 1200 West 73rd Avenue, Vancouver, British Columbia V6P 6H9, (604) 664-9324.

Serious paddlers should designate a notebook as a log for river trips. Record the river, date, flow rate, and details about the river conditions for each trip. Before long, the log will establish a pattern of flows and how they affect floating on a given river.

Incidentally, the U.S. government refers to a stream flow measuring device as a "gage." The explanation: It's easier to spell than "gauge."

Historic Flows

Knowing how much water flows through a river is worthless if a paddler has nothing by which to judge that flow. For instance, the Kettle River can be run at flows as high as 4,000 cubic feet per second. But the same flow on the Thompson River would wash out roads and make paddling ridiculously dangerous. A regional disaster would be declared if the Columbia River dropped to 4,000 cfs. At Hanford Reach, the Columbia averages 108,000 cfs—enough water to flood three rivers the size of the Spokane. By comparison, Crab Creek runs at an average of 63 cfs and goes dry some years.

Where possible, this book includes historic flow data about each river. By studying the average and record high and low flows, paddlers can put into perspective the data they've received from the USGS or Canadian sources.

Life Vests

The U.S. Coast Guard reports that 63 people died in boating accidents in 1993 in the states covered by this book. National boating organizations report that 80 percent of all people who die while boating are not wearing life vests, or personal flotation devices (PFDs).

The law and common sense demand that every canoeist have a PFD. In some jurisdictions (including Spokane County), it must be worn at all times on moving water. Most counties require that children wear life vests at all times. Besides keeping you afloat, a PFD will offer some insulation against cold water and protect your back from rocks if you're floating down a river.

The old orange PFD that is familiar to sailors has a "horse collar" that wraps around the wearer's neck, and is designed to turn an unconscious person upright in water. Trouble is, it's so bulky and uncomfortable it usually ends up decorating the floor of the canoe, floating away uselessly in a mishap. This type of PFD (labeled Type I or II by the Coast Guard) provides no protection for the wearer's back. Older models, or those that have been abused, may develop leaks and should be discarded.

If you'll be paddling only on still water, and only on calm days, a horse collar PFD may be all you need. But wind can transform placid lakes into violent waters in minutes. Many of the Northwest's best trips are on streams, and most canoeists eventually get the bug to try at least mellow whitewater. A PFD that fits like a vest (marked Type III on the Coast Guard label) is more appropriate for those situations. These PFDs are more expensive than the horse collars, and will not turn an unconscious boater upright. But they are the most comfortable of Coast Guard–approved PFDs, and allow the most freedom of movement. Therefore, they are the most likely to be worn.

Don't buy a PFD that is not Coast Guard approved.

Floats for Your Boat

Flotation devices aren't just for people. Savvy boaters have learned to fill every available spot in their canoes with flotation, in the form of strapped-in foam blocks, inner tubes, or, better yet, vinyl air bags. The bags displace water that comes into the boat while running rapids. A canoe filled with air is much more maneuverable than one filled with water. Also, a boat equipped with flotation bags is much easier to rescue and right, should it capsize.

Flotation bags come in various sizes to properly fill the bow and stern, or to contour in the rear of a kayak. They also come in different sizes to fill the entire mid-section of a canoe, or just a portion of it in order to leave room for gear.

River Hazards

A river is not static. Water levels fluctuate dramatically from season to season, or even from day to day. Storms and dam releases can cause a river to rise in minutes. Flooding, erosion, and other natural forces can cause a river to change its course. Gravel bars can disappear from one bend, only to reappear on another. Trees fall across the stream, logjams pile up, and people alter the riverbank.

Because of the changing conditions, it is imperative that paddlers remain alert and scout ahead for river hazards. This is especially true on unfamiliar waters, in wilderness areas, or anytime a dumping could lead to hypothermia. After scouting, you may decide to portage or line your boat around a rock-strewn stretch of whitewater. Scouting may reveal an easy route through the maze. Paddling blindly through the rapids only invites trouble.

"Strainers" are common river obstructions. Called "sweepers" by some boaters, these hazards are created by downed trees with branches that comb the flow without stopping it. They are most common on the outside bends of streams. Strainers can trap a boat or swimmer against the current. Avoid them.

Small dams, bridge abutments, and waterfalls create dangerous holes and undertows. A small hole downstream from a submerged rock can be a fun play area for surfing. But paddlers must learn from experienced boaters to distinguish between play waves and holes that can swamp a boat and hold it underwater.

The power of current should not be underestimated. Even slow-moving, shallow water can wrap a swamped canoe around a rock, or crush a paddler who carelessly gets caught between the boat and the obstruction.

Rating the River

Rafters, canoeists, and kayakers judge individual rapids and stretches of river according to the International Scale of River Difficulty outlined in the Safety Code of the American Whitewater Affiliation.

Class 1: Moving water with a few riffles and small waves. Few or no obstructions.

Class 2: Easy rapids with waves up to 3 feet, and wide, clear channels that are obvious without scouting. Some maneuvering is required.

Class 3: Rapids with high, irregular waves often capable of swamping an open canoe. Narrow passages that often require complex maneuvering. Requires scouting from shore.

Class 4: (Not suitable for open canoes.) Long, difficult rapids with constricted passages that often require precise maneuvering in very turbulent waters. Scouting from shore is necessary, and conditions make rescue difficult. Boaters in covered canoes and kayaks should have the ability to Eskimo roll.

Class 5: Extremely difficult, long, and very violent rapids with highly congested routes, which should always be scouted from shore. Rescue conditions are difficult, and there is significant hazard to life in the event of a mishap. Ability to Eskimo roll is essential for boaters in kayaks and decked canoes.

Class 6: Difficulties of Class 5 carried to the extreme of navigability. Nearly impossible and very dangerous. For well-equipped teams of experts only, after close study.

Be aware that judging rapids is subjective, not precise. A rafter or kayaker asked to judge a rapid may underestimate its size and hazard to canoes. A rapid judged Class 2 in July may be Class 3 or 4 during spring runoff or if the power company decides to open the dam gates upstream. Minor whitewater becomes a major hazard if strainers or other new obstructions are added. There is no shame in portaging around a Class 2 rapid if the paddler is uncomfortable running the stretch—in fact, only a fool would proceed with such reservations.

Whitewater is only one indication of a trip's difficulty. When selecting a trip, paddlers should carefully and honestly consider their ability, their familiarity with the water, and the quality of boats and safety equipment available to them. Remote trips must be judged more cautiously than those close to home and emergency assistance.

Finally, paddlers should remember the "rule of 100": Trips should be judged one class level more difficult than normal if the water and air temperature added together is 100°F or colder. (Remember, too, that such cold temperatures require wet suits or dry suits.)

Most river trips in this book are limited to Class 1 and 2 in summer and fall. Alternate routes or portages are described where larger rapids are encountered.

Cold-Weather Paddling

Some streams (and lakes, if they remain ice-free) are at their finest in the winter. Waters that were packed with water-skiers and fishermen a few months earlier are quiet in December, January, and February, especially if snow is covering the banks. Mosquitoes are absent, and wildlife may be more easily observed.

Winter paddling presents its own unique challenges. Hazards are exaggerated compared to summer. Weather can turn from calm to "interesting" to dangerous in a matter of minutes. The cold can rob your strength and coordination, and muddy your thinking. A winter dunking puts the paddler in extreme jeopardy of hypothermia. A person who is not wearing a protective suit can die in 15 to 20 minutes while immersed in water colder than 50°F. Death can come in less than 10 minutes if the water is colder than 40°F. In cold water, you may not be able to grip with your hands. The shock of cold water can stop body functions immediately.

Preparation is the key. Wear layers of polypropylene and wool clothes even on mild winter days. Strip off clothes if you start to sweat. Put on more layers if you get chilled. The outside layer ideally should be a paddler's dry suit, a rubberized jumpsuit with waterproof seals at wrists, ankles, and neck.

Stay close to shore, carry snacks and emergency equipment (including firestarter), and take a dry bag with a change of wool or pile clothing. Winter is no time to take chances.

Hypothermia

Hypothermia, which begins when the body loses heat faster than it can be produced, is a major threat to paddlers. Hypothermia is most common when the air temperature is between 30°F and 50°, but it can hit any time of year, especially if one is unprepared for a change in the weather. Damp clothes and a cool breeze can make a paddler's body temperature plummet, even if the air temperature is in the 60s. Protect yourself by wearing clothing that wicks moisture from the skin (not cotton, which absorbs and retains moisture), along with a windproof shell. Change out of wet clothes as soon as possible.

Winter canoeing on the Yakima River (Dan Hansen photo)

Signs of hypothermia include slurred speech, shivering, clumsiness, and a general inability to function properly. Victims usually don't realize they are suffering the symptoms and may become belligerent, so it is up to paddling partners to take action. Stop traveling, remove any wet clothing, and bundle the victim in a blanket or a sleeping bag. Give the victim non-alcoholic fluids. Start a fire if necessary. People suffering from hypothermia should not be massaged or warmed too quickly—either can lead to cardiac arrest in extreme cases.

Drinking Water

Dipping a cup in an icy stream is a romantic image of backcountry travel. The view through a microscope is not so idyllic. Even the clearest streams and most remote lakes can contain bacteria, viruses, and *Giardia*—a protozoan spread by the droppings of animals and the poor sanitation habits of people. Ingesting these pests can cause diarrhea, vomiting, abdominal cramps, weight loss, and other unpleasant and potentially incapacitating symptoms. The illness may show up within days or possibly not for several weeks. It will not go away without treatment.

Boiling water for several minutes will kill most microscopic pests. But boiling is inconvenient and uses extra fuel. Chlorine or iodine tablets are effective when used properly, but they take time to do the job. Because of the drawbacks, a paddler relying on boiling or chemical treatment may be tempted to drink water straight from a stream, or go long stretches without water, neither of which is advisable.

Filters are an effective water treatment system. Many excellent filters are available for less than $100, and many weigh only a few ounces.

Canoeists also have the option of bringing plastic containers or poly-bags filled with gallons of drinking water from home.

GETTING STARTED
Learning to Paddle

Paddling skills make trips safer and more fun. Good paddlers can play in whitewater that makes beginners blanch. They know how to ferry across a river to avoid the worst spots, how to slip into eddies for a break amid the fury, and how to brace a boat when it starts to tip. On lakes, proper techniques will keep the canoe straight and make the most efficient use of each stroke.

Outfitters, outdoor shops, parks departments, and canoe clubs offer classes on paddling skills and rescue techniques. If paddling courses are unavailable near your home, check out books or videos.

Selecting a Boat

Unless you can afford to buy and store a boat for every paddling situation—some paddlers have this luxury, the rest dream about it—the vessel you choose will be a compromise. This is merely a brief guide to considerations you should give to boat selection.

Canoes

Suitable for lakes or streams, canoes are available in solo or tandem. They can be paddled or poled, or powered by a small outboard motor. Designs that compromise the maneuverability of whitewater canoes with the straight-ahead efficiency of cruisers may be the best all-around boat for casual paddlers.

Some purists still paddle wooden or canvas canoes for their beauty and tradition. For the sake of durability, performance, and cost, most canoeists turn to modern materials, each of which has advantages and drawbacks. Canoes made of aluminum and Royalex ABS, a plastic composite favored by whitewater paddlers, are tough but heavy. Those made of fiberglass are lighter and more fragile. Kevlar is feather-light and stronger than fiberglass, but is more expensive than other materials and nearly impossible to repair at home.

The best advice: Rent or borrow several canoes of various styles before deciding which to own.

Kayaks

Tiny whitewater kayaks fit paddlers like a wet pair of pants and are the most maneuverable craft on the water. Whitewater kayakers can weave through rock gardens where other boaters would breach. They surf and play on waves that would flip most canoes. And, if they do flip, kayaks can be rolled upright without taking on water or spitting out the paddler.

Sea kayaks are longer and sleeker. They are stable and sealed from taking on water. This makes them ideal for big lakes or broad flatwater rivers. Kayaks are available in plastic, fabric, fiberglass, and Kevlar, and in solo or tandem models. Some kayaks can be dismantled and packed into duffel bags that can be transported on commercial airplanes.

Inflatables

Inflatables range from discarded automobile inner tubes to massive rafts with space for a family and a week's worth of gear. Inflatable canoes and kayaks are at their best on whitewater rivers. Paddling or rowing one for long distances on a lake or flatwater river—particularly in windy weather—can be a chore.

EQUIPMENT

Even if you own a war canoe, it's possible to fill every inch to the gunwales with gear. Virtually all camping and boating gear on the market is tempting. Most of it is unnecessary. Some is mandatory for all responsible boaters.

Never go into the backcountry on foot or afloat without the Ten Essentials:

1. Map of the area
2. Compass
3. Extra food
4. Extra clothing
5. Flashlight with extra cells and bulbs
6. First-aid kit
7. Matches in a waterproof case
8. Firestarter
9. Pocketknife
10. Sun protection, including sunglasses and sunscreen

In addition to PFDs for each paddler, every canoe should be equipped with grab lines attached to the bow and the stern. The lines should be made of a material that floats, and kept handy in untangled bundles under bungee cords or bicycle inner tubes.

River runners should carry a throw-bag rescue rope, and should be trained in its use. A waterproof map case allows maps to be kept handy and dry. Insect repellent will make shore time bearable.

Each canoe should carry a spare paddle, a bailer, and a sponge for soaking up hard-to-reach water that ships into the boat. A whistle—required in Idaho—will help canoeists in distress catch the attention of other boaters.

See Appendix A for an extensive gear list.

Maps

Accurate maps are vital for finding roads, bridges, river access, campgrounds, and other features. A good map, together with a compass, lets paddlers identify the mountain in the distance and tells them they are a mile from the take-out when they cross under the power lines. River travelers who want to spice their trips with hikes need maps to locate trails.

With a map, the knowledge to read it, and a little imagination, one can fill blustery winter days with visions of rivers yet unpaddled.

The casual paddler could do well in Washington, Montana, and Idaho with little more than the Gazetteer atlases published by the

DeLorme Mapping Company. Each softcover book covers an entire state. Although not detailed enough for wilderness travel, the maps show campgrounds, roads, river routes, and other features. The atlases are available in most sporting goods stores. The Southeastern British Columbia Recreational Atlas is the Canadian equivalent of the U.S. Gazetteers described above.

Many trips can be found on national forest maps, which show nearly every turn of road and river. These maps are available for a fee at United States Forest Service offices. Be aware, however, that the maps can be several years out of date, and may show secondary roads that are closed.

The United States Geological Survey (USGS) is the largest purveyor of maps in the nation. The agency's 7.5-minute topographical maps (1 inch equals about a third of a mile) are the standard for backcountry travelers. They often show river miles, and are useful for noting the location of larger rapids and waterfalls, but generally are more detailed than paddlers need. They also are awkward and expensive for river travel, since several maps may be needed to cover a single trip. The agency's 1:100,000 scale topographical maps (1 inch equals 1.6 miles) show good details of geological features. Unfortunately, roads are not labeled, so the maps must be used in conjunction with the Gazetteer or Forest Service maps.

Sources for maps are listed in Appendix D.

Paddling Clothes

Proper clothing for paddling varies as much by water temperature as by ambient air temperature. T-shirts and shorts (along with a liberal coating of sunscreen) are fine for midsummer trips if the water is warm and the weather balmy. Switch to long pants and long sleeves for thorough sun and bug protection.

Wet cotton saps warmth from a body. So, for cooler summer days, or with the cooler water of early summer and fall, switch to polypropylene, pile, wool, and similar materials that retain some warmth when wet. Carry rain gear in case of rain, snow, or wind. Winter and spring paddling require a wet suit as the first layer of clothing or a dry suit as the final layer (see Cold-Weather Paddling, earlier in this section).

A paddler's feet are nearly always wet, so keep them warm by wearing wool or pile socks (and bring extras). Avoid wearing stiff-soled shoes, such as hiking boots. Flexible soles grip better, are more comfortable when kneeling in the boat, and are not as likely to get caught under a seat during a mishap. Sneakers are a good choice for warm weather; neoprene booties or rubber-soled boots are best when the weather turns cold or nasty. Paddlers should avoid hip boots or waders, which are extremely dangerous if the canoe capsizes. However, knee-high rubber boots are a good choice in some situations.

A good, layered paddling wardrobe for cool weather would include an inner layer of polypropylene underwear, an insulating layer of synthetic pile, and a waterproof shell.

Paddlers who wear glasses should secure them with head straps or toggles.

Packing for an Overnight Trip

Paddlers are often tempted to fill their boats with every comfort one would take car-camping—folding chairs, a cast-iron skillet, a roomy tent, and an ice chest filled with beverages and fresh fruit, for instance. This is fine in most cases.

More prudent packing is warranted if your trip is long, if camp will be in a different spot each night, or if long portages are expected. In those cases, paddlers should think like backpackers, since that's what a canoeist becomes while portaging.

Experienced wilderness travelers question the need for each item. Don't take the entire tackle box if a small selection of lures will do the trick. Consider taking a pocket camera rather than a heavier SLR with a selection of lenses. Pack dried food so you can leave behind the ice chest and can opener.

Pack heavy items as low as possible to keep the canoe stable. Distribute the weight evenly from side to side and end to end. A properly loaded canoe will ride trim—that is, level from bow to stern.

Gear should be lashed to the thwarts or tie-downs so it isn't lost if the canoe tips. Dry bags and other large, light items make good flotation if they are secured so they don't rise above the gunwales when the boat is swamped.

SAVVY PADDLING

Becoming a savvy paddler is fairly simple if you learn from your mistakes. One of the first hard lessons is that gear should be secured in the canoe *every* time you launch.

Keeping Gear Dry

Gear has a way of getting wet in canoes and kayaks, even on glassy lakes. Water drips from paddles, it sloshes in with shoes, it rains down

Canoe camping under the stars on Winchester Wasteway (Rich Landers photo)

from above, and splashes over the gunwales. Eventually, whatever is on the floor of the boat will be soaked.

The waterproof dry bags sold at paddling and rafting shops are the easiest way to protect clothes and other soft items. Doubled garbage bags stuffed in a duffel or pack will work in non-whitewater situations. Experienced boaters keep a complete change of clothes, extra food, matches, and other items, such as a first-aid kit, in a small dry bag that goes with them, attached to a thwart, wherever they paddle. Items needed more frequently during a trip, such as sunscreen, camera, and snacks, can be kept in an even smaller dry bag or waterproof plastic case attached to a thwart.

Dry bags and expensive specialty cases are not the only choices. Enterprising boaters store gear in army surplus ammunition cans (equipped with rubber seals), five-gallon buckets with tight-fitting lids, plastic kitchen containers, or even the plastic jars used to ship olives to restaurants. For extra protection, place maps, toilet paper, and other small, essential items in zippered freezer bags.

Etiquette along the Water

Low-impact use of wild places has not caught on a quarter century after the first Earth Day. Anyone who visits popular lakes or streams can see the abuse: trees scarred or killed by hatchet-wielding campers; beaches littered with cigarette butts, broken glass, and fishing line.

The trips described in this book are not pristine. Enter the woods behind Upper Priest Lake's popular campsites and you'll likely see a garden of toilet paper. Visit the island at Bonnie Lake and you'll see trees burned by campers who lost control of their fire. The banks of the Spokane River are a depository for trash, yard waste, and useless home appliances—so much garbage, in fact, that paddlers have lost river access as park rangers close roads used by the vandals.

The scene could get worse as human populations increase.

Paddlers should be models in showing respect for the river, the land, the wildlife, and fellow visitors. A few guidelines:

- Leave the radio at home, and cut out needless noise. Neighboring campers will appreciate the consideration, and you'll have a better chance of seeing wildlife.
- Give anglers a wide berth.
- Get permission before crossing or camping on private property. Crawl under or through wire fences; don't climb over them. Gates that were closed when you arrived should be left that way.
- Leave the landscape as you found it, or better. Don't pick wildflowers, cut branches, or drive nails into trees.
- Restrain dogs on a leash if necessary to keep them from bothering other parties or chasing wildlife.
- Killing an occasional gamefish is fine if law allows it, and knowledgeable mycologists won't hurt anything by complementing a

meal with a few mushrooms. But living off the land along lakes and rivers nowadays is selfish and unethical.

- Hang food out of reach in trees, or secure in plastic containers to avoid attracting wild creatures into camp and tempting them to become junkies for human food.
- Don't litter. Take a garbage bag and pick up after others.
- Limit group size to a reasonable number. Exactly what is reasonable depends on the setting. Larger groups are better suited to widely used waters, rather than pristine backcountry areas. Groups of any size should use campgrounds when possible to avoid new impacts to natural shorelines.

Sanitation

Nothing is more offensive than stumbling across someone else's poor job of covering up after his or her restroom habits. On popular rivers, land managers have had no reasonable alternative but to require boaters to carry out all human waste. Even in the less crowded Inland Northwest, such rules are imminent along some waters.

Each canoeist or family should carry a small trowel and use the "cathole method" if the need arises in areas where outhouses are unavailable: Bury human waste 6 to 8 inches deep, and at least 200 feet away from water, camps, and trails. Cover the hole with the sod that was removed from it. Carry out used toilet paper in zippered plastic bags. Burn used toilet paper only if it can be done safely and completely.

Campers should use only biodegradable soap for washing themselves and dishes. The chore should be done with a bucket at least 200 feet from water. Rinsing dishes or yourself in lakes or streams degrades water quality a little at a time. Don't think of yourself as a single visitor. Remember, you are just one in a cast of thousands.

Fires

Campfires, for all their mesmerizing appeal and tradition, are a high-impact pleasure. Consider doing without one if you are camping in an area that does not have established fire rings. You'll leave a neater camp and treat yourself to a better view of the stars.

If a fire is desired, pick a campsite where a fire ring is already established. If one is not available and a fire is necessary, build it on bare earth or rock, or below the high water mark on gravel bars. Leave snags standing—they are important homes to many wildlife species and the insects they eat. Use only dead wood—preferably driftwood—

no larger in diameter than your wrist, and burn it completely. After the ashes have cooled completely, consider packing them home in a bag. At the very least, scoop the ashes and scatter or bury them away from camp or the gravel bar, then replace any sod that was removed before the fire was started.

Some backcountry paddlers use fire pans or boxes when camping where fire rings are not established. They are available through paddler supply companies, or are easily made at home (Bill Mason's book *Song of the Paddle* includes plans for a simple box made of sheet metal). They are required on some popular Western rivers.

A gas stove is the most efficient way to cook, and the easiest on the woods.

Paddling with Children

Children make wonderful traveling companions. They find delight in wonders adults have stopped noticing, and ask questions big people forget to ask: What keeps a water skipper from sinking? Why do owls say "who"? How far do the stars go?

Some parents never experience this wonder because they wait for the entire family to reach the "proper" age before hitting the water. That magical time can be elusive.

Taking the kids means adjusting your schedule to keep them happy. Don't plan on covering the same distance you would on an adult trip, or even half that distance. Instead, allow all day for a short trip, and let the children set the schedule. Take frequent shore breaks. Explore backwaters. Talk to the turtles and watch the ducklings. Attach a line to one of the child's floating toys so it can be dragged alongside the canoe. Take a bucket of river rocks to toss into the current. Most canoes don't have seats for non-paddling passengers. A dry bag stuffed with clothes, or the detachable cloth seats sold at canoe shops, are among the comfortable alternatives to forcing a child to sit on the wet canoe bottom. Give each child a personal bag of snacks and a water bottle. It helps if there are other children in companion canoes.

Likewise, the family's first overnight trip should be a short one, to a destination where the kids can explore animal tracks in the sand and take hikes with their parents. Pick a weekend when the forecasters are predicting pleasant weather. Don't be too proud to cut the trip short if the weather turns nasty. But the authors have learned that kids can find great adventure in sitting out a hail storm on a riverbank under an overturned canoe braced lean-to style with paddles.

Children must be protected from overexposure to the sun, and should be dressed more warmly than adult paddlers in chilly weather. Layered clothes and brimmed hats are key to their comfort.

Children should wear PFDs whenever they are in the canoe or near the water. A wide array is available, in sizes to fit chests as small as 15 inches. A child's PFD should have a crotch strap to keep the vest from riding up, and a "pillow" to keep the head afloat.

WILD DELIGHTS AND MISERIES

Lakes, streams, and the riparian zones that surround them are magnets for wildlife. A partial list of frequently sighted species in the Inland Northwest includes muskrats, beavers, turtles, and a variety of birds. The truly lucky might spot bears, moose, raccoons, otters, bald eagles, or loons. Even on urban waters, such as the Spokane River, visitors can expect to see ospreys, mergansers, and a variety of ducks.

The temptation is to get as close to wildlife as possible. Doing so only makes wild animals turn tail and run. In spring, this could force a bird to leave its nestlings to the ravages of a predator. In winter, disturbances force deer to waste energy. Better to keep a good distance away, and view any of these creatures, big or small, briefly through binoculars or a telephoto lens.

Consider keeping a waterproof bag or box in your boat for a "reference library" of guides to birds, reptiles, amphibians, mammals, tracks, and wildflowers.

Some flora and fauna found in the Inland Northwest are of particular interest to paddlers. Among them:

Bears: Black bears and even the rare grizzly could be encountered on some of the trips in this book. Boaters must do their part to avoid attracting either of these species. Bears that get a taste of human food often become nuisances that ultimately must be destroyed. Keep your campsite clean. Lock food and garbage in a vehicle or hang it far away from the tenting area in a tree, hoisting the food bags at least 4 feet from the trunk and 10 feet off the ground. Cook and eat far away from the tenting area, too. Pack out all garbage.

Rattlesnakes: These venomous reptiles are effective rodent exterminators, but are rarely aggressive to humans. Snakebites are almost always caused by human carelessness. Few rattlesnake strikes are fatal, but they can cause swelling, fever, and severe pain. Commercial venom extraction pumps can be effective.

Bugs: Insect repellent containing DEET is a powerful defense against the blackflies and mosquitoes that haunt paddlers. New solutions with less than 30 percent DEET are effective and safer than higher concentrations of the chemical, especially for children. Long-sleeved shirts, long pants, and a headnet provide the safest defense, and won't leave your food tasting like it was cooked in a refinery.

Ticks: Once aboard an unsuspecting host, a tick will bury its head and start sucking, sometimes passing diseases to the host. The best way to remove a tick is to catch it in the 6 or so hours before it begins to feed. Remove a feeding tick by grasping the parasite's head with a small pair of tweezers and pulling gently until it detaches.

Poisonous plants: Poison oak and poison ivy can be encountered while portaging, scouting river routes, or exploring near camp. The woody vines produce a resin that inflicts painful rashes, blisters, and swelling. Benadryl and other antihistamines, and creams containing calamine, relieve some of the itching and pain of the inflammation, which may not appear for days after exposure. Those who know they have brushed against these plants should immediately wash exposed skin with soap and water. Clothes and equipment exposed to the plants must also be washed, since the resin can remain potent for months.

Fishing

One of the joys of lake or river travel is catching fish for sport or dinner. Most manufacturers offer a variety of multi-piece rods that take up little room in a pack. A rod holder is essential for trolling. Conscientious fishers use artificial flies or lures with barbless hooks and gently release any fish that can't be eaten that day. Fish caught on bait typically swallow the hook and stand little chance of surviving if returned to the water. Catch limits and legal tackle vary from water to water and state to state, so be sure to check regulations for the area you're visiting.

ROOTS OF THE WATERS

The Inland Northwest's natural and social histories are linked by its rivers. Drainages created in the Ice Age produced salmon that attracted large gatherings of Native Americans. These same rivers became the highways for fur trading, conveyors for logging, waste dumps for mining, and the lifeblood for settlements.

The following gives but a brief overview of the waters' rich history. Paddlers can take heart in knowing that this region has been

Indians using kayaks at Pend Oreille River fishing station in 1845 near the present site of Sandpoint, Idaho (illustration by H. J. Ware, National Archives of Canada)

canoe country for thousands of years. Powerboats now dominate the waters from the Flathead to Lake Pend Oreille. But canoes and kayaks are the essence of their past.

Ice Age Floods

Glacial ice dammed the Clark Fork River about 15,000 years ago near the current site of Lake Pend Oreille. The massive natural dam built a pool up to 1,800 feet deep and spreading into portions of western Montana. When the ice dams broke, centuries of accumulated water flushed out of the lake in about 48 hours, creating the most cataclysmic flood identified on earth. The flow had 10 times more water than the combined flow of all the rivers in the world today, with water rushing to depths of about 500 feet above present day Spokane. Geologists believe similar floods occurred many times over the following centuries.

The estimated flow of the first flood was 400 million cubic feet per second. For comparison, the average peak runoff of the Spokane

River is about 24,000 cfs. The flow of the flood, rushing at about 65 mph, combined with succeeding floods caused by more ice dams, scoured the Eastern Washington landscape and left its mark for 550 miles to the Pacific Ocean. It is unclear whether humans occupied the region at that time.

The floods carved giant riverbeds. Some, such as the Spokane and Clark Fork Rivers, continue to run as rivers. Others, such as the Grand Coulee, are simply chains of lakes. The central Washington area around Lake Lenore, including Dry Falls Lake, shows classic "channeled scabland" features created by the floods. At 3 miles wide and 417 feet deep, Dry Falls would have put Niagara Falls to shame. A few miles south of Soap Lake on Highway 17, seemingly misplaced boulders stand out in fields of sagebrush. A normal river current constantly moves small sand grains and pebbles downstream. But the great floods were big enough to suspend huge boulders. Known as "erratics," these boulders were bounced downstream and deposited.

Designs in Rock

Artistic columns of basalt are scattered throughout the Columbia Basin. The color ranges from coppery to coarse black. Basalt is cooled lava that flowed throughout this region as little as 6 million years ago. The molten rock seeped out of cracks in the earth, cooled, then flowed some more. When the lava cooled and solidified, it shrank and cracked, forming horizontal layers and vertical columns that sometimes arch into elaborate designs. Classic examples of this volcanic art can be enjoyed while paddling the Palouse River, along Lakes Lenore, Hutchinson, Shiner, and many other waters in the Inland Northwest.

Spokane River: A Sorry Past

The Spokane River basin originates in an enormous fan of forested backcountry drained by the Coeur d'Alene, St. Maries, and St. Joe Rivers in Idaho. These waters collect in Lake Coeur d'Alene. The Spokane River begins at the lake's outlet, but its course in history has been altered by huge forces, both upstream and down.

The river once ran free for 110 miles to the Columbia. Annual runs of steelhead and salmon fed the Spokane Indians, who gathered below the falls in what is now the city of Spokane. Archeologists have found evidence that Native Americans congregated along the upper river, in the Spokane Valley, at least 4,500 years before the first white settlers arrived.

Volcanic artistry in basalt at Lake Lenore (Rich Landers photo)

Today, the Spokane River is tamed by seven dams. These, and other dams on the Columbia River, long ago put an end to the fish runs. The 16 miles below Post Falls is the longest stretch of free-flowing water remaining on the Spokane.

Municipal sewage plants have improved water quality by replacing most of the pipes that dumped raw waste into the river and led to a temporary ban on swimming in its waters in the 1930s. The popular Centennial Trail, which runs along the river from Riverside State Park to Coeur d'Alene, has spawned new appreciation for the water, sparked annual river cleanups, and stopped some illegal dumping.

Still, the Spokane River faces the same threats as other urban waters. Riverfront development is stripping its banks of vegetation; the city of Spokane wants to flood still more of the river by raising Upriver Dam; and biologists have detected high levels of toxic PCBs in trout.

The most insidious threat to water quality dates back to the heyday of Silver Valley mining near Wallace and Kellogg. Gold was discovered up Prichard Creek 30 years before Idaho's statehood. Miners, trappers, and traders were followed by loggers. Before Coeur d'Alene was much more than an army outpost, the boom-and-bust town of Murray was a candidate for Idaho's capital. The Enaville Resort, built during the 1880s gold rush, is a living piece of its history, although the ladies for hire are gone. What remains is a legacy of ruin.

The upper Coeur d'Alene River looks pristine because U.S. Forest Service landscape architects carefully designed most clearcuts to be out of the public eye. Fly over this headwater of the Spokane River, however, and you quickly see the patchwork of clearcuts and ribbons of roads that contour for thousands of miles through the mountains. Roads and forestry practices have contributed to steep declines of native bull trout and cutthroats.

The scene gets darker at the confluence of the South Fork, which still carries toxic metals from a century of Silver Valley mining and smeltering into Lake Coeur d'Alene and ultimately the Spokane River.

Mission Slough near the Cataldo Mission is 250 acres of marsh-lands covering the settling ponds that collected mine waste and toxic metals from the Kellogg-Wallace mines. The waters hold perch and bass and the area attracts wildlife, but the safety of the water and soils is questionable. For political reasons, it may always be under study.

Salmon Tragedy

While logging and mining hammered the Spokane River drainage from above, the coup de grace for salmon came from downstream.

The Spokane River was one of the most productive salmon streams in the entire Columbia River watershed, and home to a run of the largest chinook salmon on the Pacific coast. Perhaps a million kings, ranging 50 to 80 pounds apiece, made the journey each year. These monster salmon, along with cohos, ran the Spokane and its tributaries and fed the native populations for thousands of years. White men wiped them out in two days.

The first blow came the day in 1915 when Long Lake Dam blocked fish passage to the upper three-quarters of the Spokane River. The last hope died the day in 1939 when Grand Coulee Dam created a barrier to all fish running up the Columbia toward the mouth of the Spokane.

The wealth of what was lost to industry above and below Spokane Falls is captured in the writings of early visitors.

In 1839, the Reverend Elkanah Walker, a missionary, described a Spokane Indian fishing camp at the river's Little Falls: "It is not uncommon for them to take 1,000 in a day. It is an interesting sight to see the salmon pass a rapid. The number was so great that there were hundreds constantly out of the water."

In 1877, after fishing on Havermale Island (now Riverfront Park in downtown Spokane), Lieutenant N. Abercrombie of the U.S. Army wrote: "Caught 400 [cutthroat] trout, weighing two to five pounds apiece. As fast as we dropped in a hook baited with a grasshopper, we would catch a big trout. In fact, the greatest part of the work was catching the grasshopper."

The good news is that the mines and logging camps provided thousands of jobs, and the dams produced cheap power that attracted major industries and kept utility bills low.

The bad news: Losing the salmon wasn't worth it.

Greening of the Columbia Basin

The Ice Age floods left water paths that later were taken over by sage and cactus. The desert southwest of Moses Lake, Washington, was a wasteland of sand dunes, thorns, and coyotes. Even the essence of wetness was elusive. Waterfowl found the area inhospitable, as did the Salish Indians, who clung to the Columbia River.

The Columbia Basin Irrigation Project created another world. Once Grand Coulee Dam was built, water eventually would be pumped from the Columbia River to grow everything from corn and potatoes to green lawns and grapes for wine. But even as the once-chapped land turned green, few people could have predicted that waterfowl would flock to new "seep lakes" in the Columbia National Wildlife Refuge, or that canoeists would someday travel hundreds of miles to paddle through the desert.

The water began to flow from canals to farmland in 1951. Runoff from the fields flowed into channels that had not seen moving water for thousands of years. With help from the Bureau of Reclamation, the Winchester Wasteway was born. Named for the railroad stop where water is diverted off the East Canal, the Wasteway runs in a man-made channel to Winchester Lake near Interstate 90. From there, the Bureau merely had to bulldoze a few short channels through sand dunes to open the mostly natural waterway east of Dodson Road.

The first drips of irrigation runoff made their way east through the Wasteway to Potholes Reservoir in 1965.

Yellow-headed blackbird at Winchester Wasteway (Rich Landers photo)

Progress in Canada

Like innumerable other river valleys in North America, the vitally important wetlands of British Columbia's Creston Valley were nearly lost to development and agriculture. Historically, the Kootenay River flooded each spring, covering much of the broad valley with water. Vast flocks of waterfowl, including thousands of tundra swans, arrived each spring. But farmers diked the river, leaving many of the wetlands permanently dry. Libby Dam in Montana, as well as other dams in Canada, further controlled the floods.

In 1968, under pressure from conservationists, the provincial and federal governments ordered large portions of the valley preserved as the 17,000-acre Creston Valley Wildlife Area. Ducks Unlimited, a sportsmen's conservation group, spent $1 million building more dikes—this time to hold water in. Water is pumped into the ponds from the river and its feeder streams, artificially mimicking the floods of old.

The result is wildlife habitat, and a great paddle trip.

Farther west in British Columbia, an effort to compromise between preservation and pressure to log the southern Monashee Mountains has been less effective for Granby River. Granby Provincial Park was designated in 1995 to protect 102,110 acres of unroaded wilderness at the headwaters. The area is remarkable for a temperate rainforest of old-growth cedar and hemlock unique to British Columbia. The province has four generally recognized rainforest ecosystems. This is the only one that exists in the interior, more than 200 miles from the coast.

At first, this seemed like an impressive victory for preservation. But soon it was clear the timber industry was pushing hard to run logging roads and clearcuts up to the new wilderness boundary at every flank. The fate of the Granby River drainage is far from predictable at the time this book is being published. Granby Park was created suddenly and with few recreational amenities in the plans.

When settlers first straggled to the Grand Forks area during the late 1880s, the Granby was called the North Fork of the Kettle River. The name was officially changed to the Granby in 1915, in honor of the Quebec mining company that had built the copper smelter on the riverbanks in 1900. But the company's influence in the area was a blink of an eye compared with the life of the river. By 1919, the copper market had collapsed. The smelter was dismantled in 1920, leaving huge black slag piles as an epitaph. The dam that had been built to power the smelter was removed in the winter of 1948, freeing the river to run wild again.

Columbia Tamed

In a sense, the Inland Northwest has only one river. Every other stream, creek, and ditch is merely a tributary of the Columbia.

The modern Columbia is hardly a river at all, but a series of lakes created by engineers. In its 1,400 miles, the river is dammed thirteen times, lighting homes as far away as California and irrigating 500,000 acres.

For all the changes, one would think politicians would rush to protect the last significant free-flowing stretch of the Columbia. But as of 1997, there was strong opposition to giving "recreational" status—the least restrictive of all designations under the Wild and Scenic River Act—to 51 miles of river known as Hanford Reach. The Columbia's last major run of wild king salmon spawns beneath the Reach's White Bluffs.

Ironically, the Reach was saved from damming only because the U.S. Government selected this desolate spot in central Washington to produce plutonium during World War II and the Cold War. Dams would have flooded the nuclear reactors, which no longer operate but have caused contamination that will take decades of work and billions of dollars to contain.

The Palouse

Like the Columbia Basin, the Palouse region of eastern Washington and northern Idaho originally was leveled by volcanic forces. Geologists believe westerly winds then carried volcanic silt to the base of the Rocky Mountains. The soil piled 30 to 40 feet deep on top of the basalt in some areas. Floods that washed away the soil from the basin didn't reach the rolling hills of the Palouse, where the basalt underpinnings are revealed at places like Palouse Falls and Elberton Gorge of the Palouse River.

When the first Europeans arrived, the Palouse's 4,000 square miles were rich grasslands. French-Canadian trappers called it Le Pelouse, which translates to "grassland country." The name stuck to the region, the river, and the Native Americans who lived there. (Early settlers called the Indians' spotted horses Palouseys, which later became Appaloosa.) Territorial Governor Isaac Stevens raved about the wildflowers that stretched to the horizon.

In the past century, farmers have plowed the grasslands, creating one of the most fertile and picturesque agricultural belts in the world. Wheat yields here are twice the national average, but wildflowers and grasses are gone, along with much of the native wildlife.

HISTORY IN A NAME

The waters of the Inland Northwest have histories that range from colorful to dark. Something of their past is invariably reflected in their geographical names. Commonly the names stem from thousands of years of Native American heritage. More often, they derive from early white explorers, trappers, settlers, and missionaries. William Clark, of the Lewis and Clark Expedition, is the namesake for the Clark Fork

River. The Thompson River is named for Canadian fur trader David Thompson, who left the most detailed early written accounts of this region. Thompson did not name the rivers after himself or friends. He preferred naming them for the tribes that lived along them.

The region's French-Canadian influence is evident in names like Coeur d'Alene, which means "awl-" or "needle-hearted." The trappers apparently gave the name to the Indians for their shrewd trading practices, and it later was transferred to the lake, town, and river. "Pend Oreille" meant "hanging ears" and "Nez Perce" meant "pierced nose," although some historians say neither tribe wore jewelry in their ears or noses. Likewise, the Flathead Indians did not flatten the heads of their children, as some coastal Northwest tribes did.

Priest Lake was named for Father Johan Roothaan, a missionary who never saw the pristine mountain lake. Father Pierre DeSmet named it Roothaan Lake after his friend and fellow Jesuit sometime in the 1840s. But Indians had difficulty pronouncing it and whites could not spell it. Even after the name eventually evolved to Priest Lake, Indians preferred their word, "Kaniksu," which means "black robe." Kaniksu remains on the region's maps as the name of the national forest that surrounds the Priest Lake area. The Catholic influence also is obvious in the names St. Joe and St. Maries.

In recent years the Yakama Indians have changed the spelling of their tribal name. But the river, county, and city all retain the old spelling, "Yakima."

Native Americans did indeed trap fish at Fishtrap Lake, or so the man who named the lake believed.

While many places are named for Indians, most of the descriptive place names coined by the tribes have not survived, often for disappointing reasons. The river now known as the Little Spokane was called the "Salmon Trout River," but the stream holds few trout and no salmon or steelhead today.

The Columbia was the "Big River" before an explorer from Boston named it for his boat.

Fork Dilemma

Deciding which fork to use for your salad in a fancy restaurant is easy compared to figuring out which fork is which on the upper Coeur d'Alene River. The history of the name discrepancy is lost, and the issue is minor unless you read maps literally.

The Coeur d'Alene National Forest map and U.S. Geological Survey maps show the Coeur d'Alene River north of Interstate 90 as having two forks—the North Fork and the South Fork. People who live in this region, however, refer to three forks, calling the Coeur d'Alene River above I-90 the North Fork. What the Forest Service map lists as the North Fork—the stream that meets the main channel about 5 miles north of Enaville—is locally known as the Little North Fork.

In the late 1980s, Idaho Fish and Game Department fishing regulations began to go along with locals, referring to the three stems as the Little North Fork, North Fork, and South Fork. Thus, the agency assumed the politically safe course that maps are wrong and people are right.

In this book, the authors stand by the maps.

Creek with Two Names

Hangman Creek is perhaps the most confusing name for waters covered in this book. Some people call it Hangman, while others call it Latah (LAY-tah). Both names have been official. But the issue has been controversial since the 1800s.

The earliest recorded name for the creek resembled the sound of Latah. Some historians believe it's a corruption of "Lartow," used in Lewis and Clark Expedition diaries to describe the area where Indians

Big Rock Hole on Hangman Creek (Rich Landers photo)

camped and fished near the Spokane River. The name also appeared as "Lahtoo" in some accounts. However, early surveyors and map makers began naming it Camas Prairie Creek.

In 1858, Colonel George Wright ordered the hanging of six to eight Indian leaders, including Chief Qualchan, partly in retaliation for the killing of troops led by Colonel Edward Steptoe. The hangings took place along the creek near Waverly in front of numb-struck tribal members who thought they'd come to make peace. Almost immediately, people began referring to the stream as Hangman Creek.

Public debates over the name still come and go. The Washington Legislature passed a resolution for the name to be changed to Latah Creek in 1899. The U.S. Board of Geographic Names officially recognized the change to Latah Creek in 1904, but has waffled on the action ever since. Although the board has a copy of the Legislature's 1899 law, it also has a letter dated 1904 from the Washington secretary of state, who wrote, "I am unable to find any act of the Legislature regarding the name Latah Creek."

Newspaper accounts indicate the debate flared in the early 1930s, with letter writers arguing that "Hangman" was an inconsiderate reminder of the slayings. Others said the reminder is necessary to prevent a cowardly incident from being forgotten. Although most maps refer to the creek and its valley as Hangman, the Spokane County Commission in 1997 voted to call the creek Latah in all official county documents. However, the Washington Board of Geographic Names rejected the county's official name change petition that same year.

Origins of Other Notable Names

Grande Ronde: Miners called it the Clay River because of its springtime color. But the name that stuck came from French-Canadian fur traders, who were more taken by the river's huge U-shaped valley: the "great round."

Kettle Falls: "Les Chaudieres" (The Kettles) was the name French-Canadian fur traders gave in the late 1800s to the falls on the Columbia River 2 miles downstream from the mouth of what fur traders later called the Kettle River. The name refers to the bowl-shaped holes scoured in the streambed below the falls.

Kootenai: (Spelled "Kootenay" in Canada.) From an Indian word meaning "water people."

Lenore: Columbia Basin historians do not know the origins of the name of this Grant County lake, created and named in 1932 after State Highway 17 split Alakali Lake in two.

Lochsa: Derived from the Nez Perce word for "rough water," given to the Idaho river that joins the Selway to form the Middle Fork of the Clearwater River.

Methow: Evolved through the white man's pronunciations of "Smeetheowe," an Indian tribe that ranged near the river. The tribe was chronicled as Smeetheowe by fur trader David Thompson in 1811. The word apparently means "sun," appropriate for the Methow Valley, which typically gets clear skies in the rain shadow of the North Cascades.

Selway: Derived from the Nez Perce word for "good canoeing."

Similkameen: "Treacherous waters" to Native Americans.

Slocan: Derived from a Canadian Indian word meaning "pierce, strike on the head." It refers to the Indian practice of spearing kokanee salmon, which used to be plentiful in the region.

Spokane: Most authorities agree the name derives from a Salish Indian word meaning "sun people," the tribe that gathered to fish for salmon near the Spokane Falls.

Walla Walla: Indian term for "place of many waters."

Wenatchee: Derived from Indian reference "We-na-tcha" or "We-na-tchi," meaning "river coming from the canyon." In 1805, Lewis and Clark used the word "Wahnahchee" in referring to this location. The name was used for the Indian tribe that lived in the valley and fished for the river's salmon.

Yaak: Derived from the Kootenai Indian word for "bow."

ACCESS: YOU CAN'T BOAT WITHOUT IT

The map of the Similkameen River Valley showed federal land coming to the edge of the road in several places. A 4-foot sign posted by a local rancher said otherwise: "No public land either side of road. No Trespassing." And while a state biologist had assured a group of paddlers there was public access to the river, no signs led the way. Sorry, said the polite woman in the ranch house, the biologist was wrong.

Turns out there are two places in the valley where the public can legally walk or drive to the edge of the river, and one of them is within sight of the rancher's doorstep. The state had bought easements from locals who apparently changed their minds about sharing the river with outsiders who might object to the destruction of stream banks or cattle defecating in the river. The Fish and Wildlife Department puts up signs and the landowners tear them down. As fewer and fewer people use the river, there is less urgency to put the signs back up. Thus, the public loses access to another river, and the river loses an advocacy group that might raise a fuss over further degradation.

It's happening all over the West.

On most rivers and lakes, paddlers are within their rights so long as they are floating atop the water or standing in it. Washington State law, for instance, gives the public the right to travel below the "ordinary high water mark." But there are exceptions.

Government officials in Washington's Ferry and Stevens Counties insist that the entire Kettle River belongs to the landowners on either side of it. Visitors can float on the water, but are trespassing if they touch the riverbed or step onto dry ground. More than one group of canoeists has been chased from beaches by landowners.

High Court Decision

In 1900, the Washington Supreme Court ruled the Little Spokane River—which had been used as a transportation route by generations of Native Americans and trappers—was non-navigable since it was not big enough "for some purpose useful to business." The ruling gave property owners the right to stop public use of the river where it flows through their land. For the next seven decades, canoeists, fishermen, and hunters routinely were cited for trespassing. The conflict subdued only because the state and Spokane County acquired land surrounding the last 7.5 miles of the river. Still, boaters upstream from the natural area are ruled by the old law.

The navigability issue rose again in 1983, when the public came close to losing access to Bonnie Lake, along with the publicly owned island in the lake's center. A hunting club that leased the private land surrounding the lake chased away boaters, warning they could be charged with trespassing if they used Rock Creek, the only access to the lake. Whitman County officials backed the boaters, claiming the creek bed as a public corridor through private land. Since then, public access has not been challenged.

Other impediments to river access lack legal backing but are just as effective. The Colville River is not included in this book partly because farmers have strung fencing across the stream in several places.

Further losses are nearly certain as landowners demand the right to control not just the activities on their property, but those on public waterways. River users can fight back by reporting illegally blocked land, and urging their legislators and state agencies to obtain more access. Perhaps most importantly, paddlers must show themselves to be good stewards of the land—picking up after themselves and others, and camping with minimal impact—so property owners have less ammunition to use against them.

A FINAL WORD ABOUT SAFETY

No guidebook can alert a reader to every possible hazard, flow rate, weather factor, or water condition. Nor can a book anticipate the specific abilities or limitations of every paddler who takes to a canoe or kayak. The descriptions in this book are not acknowledgments that every trip is safe for everyone.

River channels frequently change for reasons such as flooding and other natural or human-caused forces. The accuracy of this book cannot be guaranteed by the authors or the publisher.

Paddlers who embark on a trip mentioned in this book should read the entire introduction as well as the trip description. Make contact with appropriate agencies to check on current access considerations and water conditions. It is essential to study the topographical maps. Paddlers must choose the appropriate craft for the water and the skill levels of those who will navigate them. Important decisions must be made by scouting and evaluating the variables before launching. Anyone taking to the water must be the final judge and assume the risks and responsibility for the safety of everyone in the group.

WASHINGTON

1 • Similkameen River

Distance	•	13 miles
Time	•	5 hours
Season	•	Generally April
Shuttle	•	13.5 miles, pavement
Rating	•	Class 1; Class 2 lower 5 miles
Hazards	•	Rapids on final 5 miles
Information	•	Washington Fish and Wildlife Department in Ephrata
Maps	•	USGS Palmer, Oroville, plus Okanogan National Forest map

Few places accessible by road are as remote as the Similkameen River in north central Washington. The arid valley once attracted miners. Now, only a few ranchers and orchardists survive, with visitors coming to fish the lakes in spring or hunt mule deer in fall. The river itself is largely overlooked, since fishing is poor and access tough.

The Similkameen originates near British Columbia's Manning Park. After being joined by the Pasayten River, which flows from Washington's Pasayten Wilderness, the Similkameen runs 126 miles to the confluence with the Okanogan River. Provincial Highway 3 was built along the river for virtually its entire course in Canada. The relatively short stretch of river in Washington is roughly paralleled by a smaller road.

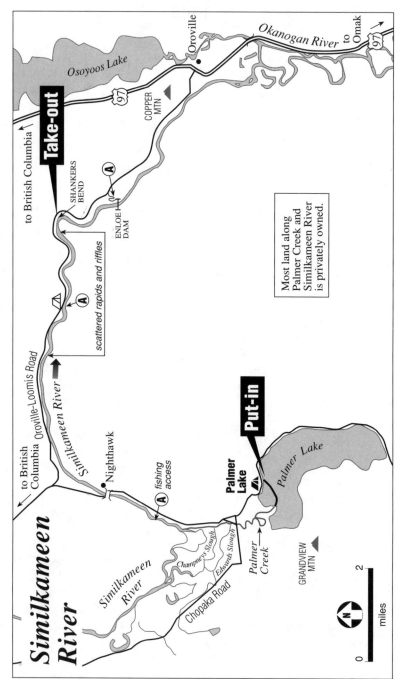

Similkameen River

Okanogan River

to Omak

97

Oroville

Osoyoos Lake

97

COPPER MTN

Take-out

to British Columbia

SHANKERS BEND

ENLOE DAM

Ⓐ

scattered rapids and riffles

Oroville–Loomis Road

to British Columbia

Similkameen River

Ⓐ

Put-in

Nighthawk

Ⓐ fishing access

Palmer Lake

Palmer Lake

Most land along Palmer Creek and Similkameen River is privately owned.

Similkameen River

Champneys Slough

Edwards Slough

Palmer Creek

Chopaka Road

GRANDVIEW MTN

N

0   2
miles

This trip takes paddlers from Palmer Lake, down its sluggish outlet creek, and into a river that starts out broad and smooth, but gains speed and excitement. The final 5 miles are accented with Class 1–2 rapids. For best paddling, look for flows of about 2,000 cubic feet per second.

ACCESS

The most obvious place to end the trip is Enloe Dam, about 3.5 miles west of Oroville on Oroville-Loomis Road. An unmarked dirt road that leads to the dam is suitable only for sturdy vehicles with high clearance. The rough, narrow access road drops about 300 feet in a mile.

The trip described here ends 1.5 miles upstream from the dam at Shankers Bend, where Oroville-Loomis Road comes close to the river. Parking for several cars is available in a dirt turnout on the opposite side of the road from the river (look for the graffiti-covered section of a concrete irrigation canal). A rough trail leads about 100 feet to the water.

To reach the put-in, continue west on Oroville-Loomis Road for 12 miles to a small Department of Natural Resources campground at the north end of Palmer Lake.

Two alternative accesses include a difficult-to-spot Fish and Wildlife Department fishing access 1.5 miles upstream from the community of Nighthawk and an informal campsite 4.5 miles downstream from Nighthawk.

PADDLE ROUTE

Flow information • USGS Water Resources in Spokane
River gauge • 12442500 near Nighthawk
Historic flows • Average 1,649; maximum 45,800; minimum 65

From the Department of Natural Resources' Palmer Lake campground, it's a short paddle to Palmer Creek. Watch for loons on this lovely lake and mountain goats on Grandview Mountain over the western shore. The creek itself meanders 3 miles through a flat, broad cow pasture, where farmers long ago placed car bodies along the banks to prevent erosion. The creek serves as an outlet stream for most of the year, but reverses itself in spring, as the Similkameen rises. At those times, Palmer Lake has two inlet creeks and no outlet. As the lake rises, it overflows onto the pasture at its north end. The lake holds smallmouth bass.

From its confluence with Palmer Creek, the Similkameen runs sluggish for about 5 miles before growing steeper, swifter, and narrower.

Prime flows on the Similkameen River (Dan Hansen photo)

Rock gardens are common. Canoes will scrape bottom when the flow is much less than 2,000 cfs. Paddlers can avoid most of the rapids by taking out at the informal campsite about 6.5 miles downstream from the confluence of the creek and river. The site also can be used as a put-in for a quick trip through the roughest water.

Shankers Bend, where the trip ends, is the start of the 70-acre pool created by Enloe Dam. More than 100 feet tall, the dam generated a small amount of power for about 50 years before it was abandoned by the Okanogan County Public Utility District in 1959. Environmental groups concerned with the return of salmon runs have suggested dismantling the dam. The deep gorge below the dam has Class 3 rapids.

2 · Methow River
(Winthrop to Twisp)

Distance	• 11 miles
Time	• 2–4 hours
Season	• Virtually year-round
Shuttle	• 8 miles, pavement
Rating	• Class 1-plus
Hazards	• Diversion dam across river; strainers
Information	• Forest Service Visitor Center in Winthrop
Maps	• USGS Winthrop, Blue Buck Mountain, Twisp East, plus Okanogan National Forest map

In 89 miles from its sources in the North Cascades, the Methow River offers something for every paddling skill level on its way to the confluence with the Columbia River near Pateros. Commercial rafting companies and skilled whitewater paddlers flock to the Class 3 and Class 4 water in the Black Canyon below Carlton. More casual paddlers tend to look farther upstream, where pristine waters originating in the Pasayten and Chelan-Sawtooth Wilderness Areas don't rumble quite so violently.

The Methow (pronounced MET-how) upstream from Winthrop weaves through a scenic valley, small ranches, and towering cottonwoods. The only drawbacks for paddlers are the high odds of encountering logjams, which are especially dangerous in high flows.

This trip winds through the gentle portion of valley downstream from Winthrop. The shores are lined with ponderosa pines and cottonwoods towering above willows, serviceberry, and bitterbrush. Strainers are always a possibility, but the likelihood of logjams is much lower than in the stretch upstream from Winthrop.

The Methow from Winthrop to Twisp has two rapids ranging to nearly Class 2, depending on flow. Bald eagles, ducks, and deer are regularly seen along the river in winter and spring. Anglers can catch rainbow trout. Some steelhead run upriver in fall.

Access

Two good put-ins are available in Winthrop. One is at the Red Barn Community Park just across the U.S. Highway 20 bridge on the upstream side of town. If flows are low, the better put-in is at the gauging station near the Highway 20 bridge on the downstream end of town. The parking area is on the downstream side of the bridge, river-left.

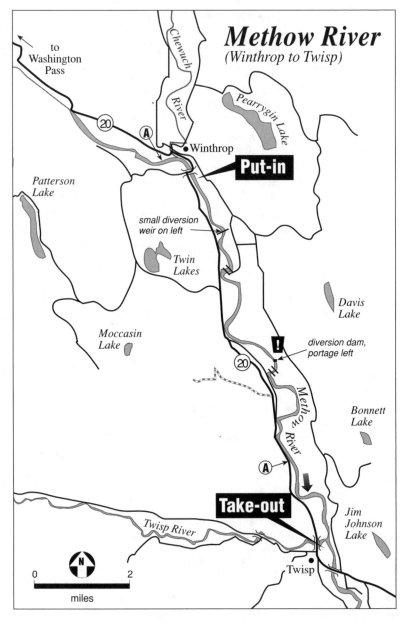

Methow River
(Winthrop to Twisp)

to Washington Pass

Chewuch River

Pearrygin Lake

● Winthrop

Put-in

Patterson Lake

small diversion weir on left

Twin Lakes

Davis Lake

Moccasin Lake

diversion dam, portage left

!

Bonnett Lake

Methow River

Take-out

Twisp River

Jim Johnson Lake

● Twisp

0   2
miles

To reach the take-out, drive south from Winthrop on Highway 20 about 8 miles to Twisp. Just south of the bridge over the Twisp River, turn east between the Road House Diner and the Chevron service station (the unmarked street is called Twisp Avenue), and drive to the second stop sign. Turn left into Twisp Community Park. Scout the best spot for a take-out.

PADDLE ROUTE

Flow information • USGS Water Resources in Spokane
River gauge • 12448500 at Winthrop
Historic flows • Average 1,072; maximum 24,400; minimum 134

The Methow River can be floated most of the year, but low water can assure bottom-bouncing in the upper stretches in August and September and portions of winter when flows dip below 300 cubic feet per second. Occasional surges in February can make great winter floating. Runoff generally peaks between mid-May and early June, with flows around 6,300 to 10,000 cfs. Paddling is not advised during peak flow levels. At any flow level, even the easier stretches of river demand that paddlers have skills to handle a few sharp turns and eddylines.

Development of scattered private homes along the river accelerated in the 1990s. Unfortunately, there is little public land above the high-water mark.

Methow River near Winthrop in February (Rich Landers photo)

A diversion dam spans the river 5 miles downstream from Winthrop. To paddlers, the dam shows up in the distance as a perfectly straight line of water from bank to bank with concrete fixtures on each side. Portage river-left. With careful scouting at some flow levels, canoeists can paddle over the diversion dam slightly left of center, but they must negotiate dangerous rocks and standing waves just below the dam. In low flows, paddlers can step out of their boats on river-right and line down over the wooden diversion.

The Methow Valley has several campgrounds managed by the Okanogan National Forest as well as at Pearrygin Lake State Park. Late-summer visitors can reap the harvest of fruit orchards that line the lower stretches of the river.

Another good paddle trip, with water ranging to Class 2, runs 12.5 miles from Twisp downstream to the fishing access off Highway 20 in Carlton. This stretch has no diversion dam to negotiate, but some stretches can be challenging, depending on the flow. USGS maps needed for that section are Twisp East and Methow.

3 • White River

Distance	•	7 miles
Time	•	2–4 hours
Season	•	Generally April through October
Shuttle	•	3 miles, pavement
Rating	•	Flatwater
Hazards	•	Deadheads, strainers, or logjams; weir near mouth of river; wind on Lake Wenatchee
Information	•	Lake Wenatchee Ranger Station
Maps	•	USGS Lake Wenatchee, plus Wenatchee National Forest map

The White River ends on a quiet note at Lake Wenatchee, understating its wild run and lofty beginnings from one of Washington's most impressive volcanic peaks. The river is named for the pulverized rock from the White River Glacier on the south flank of 10,541-foot Glacier Peak. This "glacial flour" colors the water during summer, but the stream clears when winter weather chills the glacial drip and the river is fed mostly by groundwater and snowmelt.

The upper reaches of the river are wild, as the stream plunges about 3,000 feet in elevation in 15 miles through the Glacier Peak Wilderness.

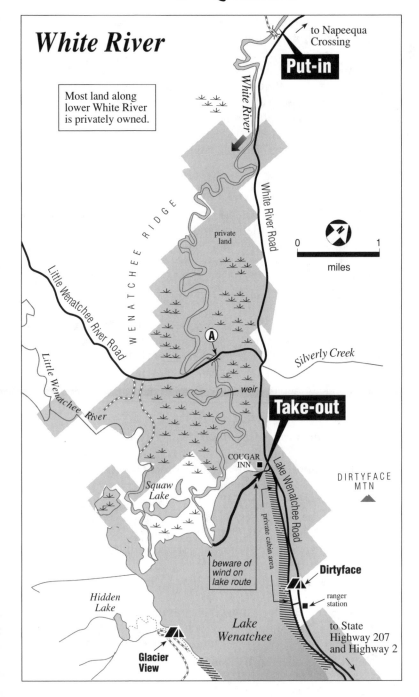

White River

Most land along lower White River is privately owned.

to Napeequa Crossing

Put-in

White River

White River Road

private land

0   1

miles

Little Wenatchee River Road

W E N A T C H E E   R I D G E

Little Wenatchee River

(A)

Silverly Creek

weir

Take-out

COUGAR INN

Lake Wenatchee Road

Squaw Lake

DIRTYFACE MTN

private cabin area

beware of wind on lake route

Hidden Lake

Dirtyface

ranger station

Lake Wenatchee

Glacier View

to State Highway 207 and Highway 2

But soon after it tumbles over White River Falls, the river mellows to the temperament of a spring creek. Cedars loom over the water for a while before giving way to towering cottonwoods.

The stretch from Sears Creek to Wenatchee Lake can be enjoyed as early as paddlers can slide a boat down the snowbanks to the water. The season lasts as late in the fall as the ice and snow allow. The area offers plenty of hiking, plus sailboarding and other recreation at Lake Wenatchee. The last week of September or first week of October is prime time to see the brilliant fall color display on this stretch of the White River.

ACCESS

From U.S. Highway 2 about 16 miles northwest of Leavenworth, Washington, turn north (near milepost 85) onto State Highway 207 toward Lake Wenatchee State Park. Cross the Wenatchee River, then bear left at a fork, where Highway 207 ends and becomes Lake Wenatchee Road. Drive to Cougar Inn, which is 9.8 miles from Highway 2. Check with lodge owners regarding parking and about using the beach as a take-out.

To reach the put-in, continue northwest on Lake Wenatchee Road for a half mile. Turn right at a fork onto White River Road (Forest Service Road 6400). (The left fork becomes Little Wenatchee River Road.) Drive 2.5 miles on White River Road to the put-in at the bridge for Sears Creek Road (Forest Service Road 6404).

PADDLE ROUTE

Although the surrounding area is managed by the Wenatchee National Forest, most land along this float is privately owned. In summer and fall, sandbars provide room for shore breaks.

The work of beavers is obvious along the river, and the banks are tree-lined and steep in many areas. Blowdown trees are common. These "strainers" can be dangerous. Always be on the watch for logjams around bends. The river generally flows slowly enough so, if it is necessary, boaters can ferry to shore and portage with little difficulty.

A weir near the mouth of the river causes a riffle during high flows. During low flows, floaters may have to line boats over the minor structure.

The biggest challenge can be the wind that crops up regularly on Lake Wenatchee. A contingency plan if you encounter a big wind is to pull out at the Little Wenatchee River Road bridge. The flow is gentle enough here to paddle downstream to the mouth and back upstream if necessary.

Other potential take-out points include the Forest Service's Glacier View Campground just south of the White River mouth, and Lake Wenatchee State Park, a 5-mile open-water paddle down to the east end of the lake.

Foggy float on White River in April (Rich Landers photo)

The Cougar Inn has upscale food and lodging. Lake Wenatchee State Park has an excellent campground with showers.

The White River attracts a run of sockeye salmon in August and September, plus some chinook salmon and steelhead. It also holds rainbows and cutthroats and the increasingly rare bull trout.

For a side trip, consider driving to White River Falls campground, about 10 miles upstream from the Forest Service ranger station. An unofficial trail leads down to an overlook of the falls, which block passage for fish as well as paddlers. Other access to the falls is via the trailhead north of the campground at the end of White River Road. Hike south on Panther Creek Trail 1522.

4 · Wenatchee River

Distance	•	10 miles
Time	•	3 hours
Season	•	Generally March through July
Shuttle	•	9 miles, pavement
Rating	•	Class 1; avoidable Class 2-plus
Hazards	•	Bridge abutments, changing river channels, rapids; wind at confluence with Columbia
Information	•	Wenatchee Chamber of Commerce
Maps	•	USGS Cashmere, Monitor, Wenatchee, plus Wenatchee National Forest map

No one should be surprised that the Wenatchee River is perhaps the most popular floating stream in Washington. The 54-mile river is like a paddler's WalMart, offering most everything one could want with cheap convenience. Various stretches range from flatwater to violent whitewater. Tributaries such as the Chiwawa spice up the action for experts. A four-lane highway parallels the lower Wenatchee, making shuttles a whiz. Backpacking destinations in the alpine areas above the river are so popular, the Wenatchee National Forest's Leavenworth ranger station conducts lottery drawings for trail permits. The area is studded with national forest and state park campgrounds.

That's just a sampling of the attractions. Flowing down into the rain shadow on the east side of the North Cascades, the Wenatchee is a destination for hordes of paddlers and rafters escaping the dreary weather in Western Washington. Conversely, locals flock to the river to seek relief from the sunny weather that has made the Wenatchee area a hotbed for the orchard industry.

Numerous commercial rafting companies as well as kayakers prefer the Class 3–4 whitewater stretch from Leavenworth to Cashmere. Just upstream from Leavenworth, the river constricts into Tumwater Canyon, a violent bouldered channel that rates Class 5 or worse.

Canoeists can find more Class 2 paddling from the source of the river at Lake Wenatchee downstream to Plain. This stretch is accessible by paved road, but has a more forested and remote nature than the lower river. More Class 2 can be found from Plain downstream to Tumwater Campground, the last possible take-out before entering the dangerous water of Tumwater Canyon.

The trip described here, from Cashmere to Wenatchee, generally rates as easy during moderate flows. Some sections of waves and rapids provide challenges for those who want them, but less experienced paddlers can avoid difficulty in most conditions, with the exception of peak spring flows that normally occur sometime in May.

Surfing a Class 2-plus rapid below Wenatchee River County Park (Rich Landers photo)

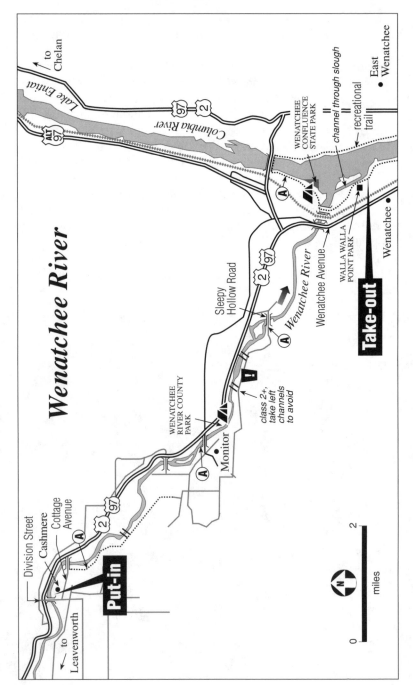

Wenatchee River

to Chelan

Lake Entiat

Columbia River

97 2

ALT 97

WENATCHEE CONFLUENCE STATE PARK

channel through slough

recreational trail

East Wenatchee

Ⓐ

WALLA WALLA POINT PARK

Wenatchee Avenue

Wenatchee River

2 97

Sleepy Hollow Road

Wenatchee

Ⓐ

Take-out

WENATCHEE RIVER COUNTY PARK

Monitor Ⓐ

❗ class 2+, take left channels to avoid

2 97

Division Street
Cashmere
Cottage Avenue

Ⓐ

Put-in

to Leavenworth

N

0   1   2
miles

ACCESS

The put-in is west of Wenatchee. From U.S. Highway 2/97 at Cash-mere, Washington (milepost 112), exit south at the stoplight onto Cottage Avenue. Cross the bridge over the Wenatchee River. Turn right onto Maple Street (at Village Inn Motel). Continue straight to the put-in at Riverside City Park. (For an alternate put-in that is best in low flows, enter Cashmere on Cottage Avenue, cross the bridge over the river and immediately turn left onto Riverfront Drive. Go 0.2 mile to an undeveloped put-in across from a power substation.)

To reach the take-out, drive east on four-lane Highway 2/97, fol-lowing the exit signs to Wenatchee. The highway bends south and becomes Wenatchee Avenue at the north end of Wenatchee. Turn east (toward the Columbia River) at the stoplight onto Hawley Street, which bends right and becomes Miller Street. Turn right (south) on Walla Walla Street toward Eagle Hardware. Then turn left (east) into Walla Walla Point Park (open 6:00 A.M. to midnight; no camping allowed). Take the left fork on the park access road and leave a vehicle in a parking slot near the restrooms. The take-out is by the footbridge over the inlet to the cove.

Other access points in this stretch include:

- Fishing access on the upstream, river-right side of the bridge at Monitor. From Highway 2/97, turn south on lower Sunnyslope road (between mileposts 117 and 118) then right on Sleepy Hol-low Road to the access at the bridge.
- Wenatchee River County Park, near Monitor, off Highway 2/97 at milepost 115.
- Boat launch at end of Orondo Street in Wenatchee.
- Wenatchee Confluence State Park boat launch just north of Wenatchee River mouth.

PADDLE ROUTE

Flow information • Chelan County Public Utility District
River gauge • 12462500 at Monitor
Historic flows • Average 3,205; maximum 45,900; minimum 208

Floods, such as the 40,000 cubic feet per second event in 1995, can make big changes in the lower Wenatchee River by creating new chan-nels. Keep this in mind as you read this description, and as you paddle the river from year to year.

Ideal flows for paddling range from 1,500–6,000 cfs. Lower flows expose too many rocks. Flows higher than about 8,000 cfs create swift currents with water flooding into the shoreline brush, erasing eddies and posing bigger consequences for little mistakes. Getting off the river could be difficult if you dump in high flows.

Several islands force paddlers to make route choices. One channel generally is better than another, but this can change from year to year. Paddlers must make the call on a given day. Virtually all sharp river bends—especially those against riprapped banks—have larger waves that can be run for fun or avoided by keeping tight to the inside shore.

The second of seven bridges you'll pass under on this trip is at Monitor. Just downstream from Monitor is a good pit stop at Wenatchee River County Park on river-left.

Pay particular attention to Class 2-plus rapids in the right channel of the island just downstream from the county park. (The rapids can be scouted before launching from Sleepy Hollow Road on the south side of the river.) To avoid the rapids, take the left or center channel at the island. The left channel has a sharp turn and a possibility of strainers. The center channel is likely to be the clearest option.

Just before the confluence with the Columbia, look for a channel into the trees on river-right after passing under a series of three bridges. The channel offers a wind-sheltered route through a slough toward the take-out. The area is a refuge for wildlife, particularly birds, waterfowl, and muskrats. At the end of the slough, paddle out through an opening into the Columbia. The big river is a reservoir here, backed up behind Rock Island Dam. Turn right and go a short way before paddling under the footbridge to the take-out cove at Walla Walla Point Park.

Anglers should check state regulations for special seasons on hatchery-raised salmon and steelhead.

5 • Lake Lenore

Distance	•	9 miles round trip
Time	•	2–5 hours
Season	•	Generally March through November
Shuttle	•	None
Rating	•	Flatwater
Hazards	•	Wind
Information	•	Washington Fish and Wildlife Department in Ephrata
Maps	•	USGS Banks Lake, Moses Lake, plus Grant County map

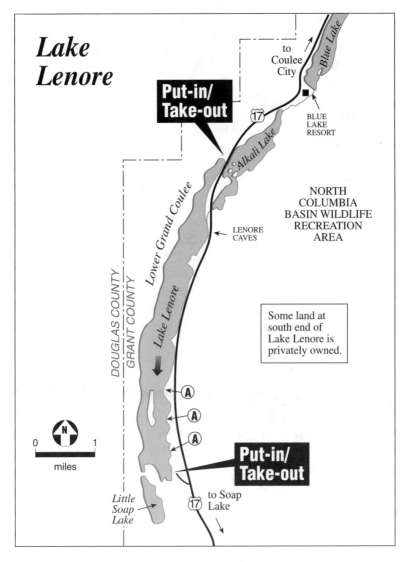

Here's a place to catch a whopper cutthroat trout while paddling the path of great Ice Age floods that carved Grand Coulee roughly 15,000 years ago.

Lake Lenore is 4 miles long, bordered on the east by Highway 17 and on the west by cliffs that drop precipitously more than 1,200 feet from the coulee rim. The weather tends to be warmer here than at the eastern and western edges of Washington, making this a particularly pleasant destination in fall and early spring. Anglers will be pleased to know that these choice periods also coincide with the best fishing for the large Lahontan cutthroat trout, which can weigh up to 6 pounds. Summer can be hot here, making early morning and late evening the best times for paddling or fishing.

The lake is popular with anglers, but remains quiet since laws prohibit boats with gas motors. The Washington Fish and Wildlife Department also enforces catch limits and gear requirements that are much more restrictive than in the state's general fishing waters. Check the fishing regulations pamphlet for details. The Lahontan cutthroat trout is an import from Nevada. The high alkalinity of Lenore left the lake fishless until biologists learned that the Lahontans were specially adapted to these waters.

ACCESS

Lake Lenore is easy to reach on U.S. Highway 17 heading north from Moses Lake or heading south from the junction with U.S. Highway 2 west of Coulee City, Washington. From this junction, drive south on Highway 17 about 16 miles (to milepost 80.2) and turn west on an unmarked dirt track that winds down to a put-in or take-out point at the south end of Lake Lenore. The access at the north end is at milepost 84.8.

When driving south on Highway 17 from Coulee City, be sure to take note of several other attractions. The Dry Falls overlook is 2 miles south of the Highway 2 junction. The entrance to fine camping at Sun Lakes State Park can be found 3.7 miles south of the junction. The access road to the archeological sites at Lenore Caves is near the north end of Lake Lenore on the opposite (east) side of the highway. A rocky trail leads past shallow depressions where nomadic cave dwellers sought shelter thousands of years ago.

Additional access is available at four points on the lake's east shore, including three access points along a 1-mile stretch north of the southern put-in.

PADDLE ROUTE

Launch at either end of the lake, depending on the wind, and hug the west shore, where there are no roads, trails, or development along the cliffs. The lake generally is ice-capped from December through February. Spawning cutthroat trout become visible along the shoreline in March and April, particularly at the north end of the lake.

Most of the land around the lake is public, managed by the state or the U.S. Bureau of Reclamation. However, some private land development has occurred, notably at the south end of the lake. Anglers congregate at the north and south ends, leaving the scenic middle of the lake mostly deserted. Listen for chukar partridges clucking in the cliffs above.

At several points, paddlers can pull boats out onto the rocks and scramble up scree slopes to plateaus midway up the cliffs for good views. Watch for rattlesnakes.

Other than a few outhouses, no services are found on Lenore. Camping resorts are found at several nearby lakes.

6 • Yakima River Canyon

Distance	•	19 miles
Time	•	6 hours
Season	•	Virtually year-round
Shuttle	•	20 miles, pavement
Rating	•	Class 1-plus
Hazards	•	Heavy wind; strainers, scattered rapids
Information	•	Bureau of Land Management in Spokane
Maps	•	USGS Ellensburg South, Kittitas, Wymer

Since 1990, catch-and-release regulations have transformed the Yakima River into one of the most productive trout streams in the Northwest. Born in the snowfields of the Cascades, the stream runs swift and cold. It is home to large caddis flies and stone flies that produce trout as strong as Ellensburg stallions.

The Yakima originates east of Snoqualmie Pass at Keechelus Lake and flows 215 miles to the confluence with the Columbia River near Richland.

One need not be an angler to appreciate the river and the arid canyon that guides its route between the cities of Ellensburg and Yakima. Slowing after its fall from the mountains, the water runs gently at the base of steep, open slopes where bighorn sheep sometimes are seen, and chukar partridges can be heard laughing at weak-legged mortals. Those who come to the canyon in winter are likely to spot bald eagles. Spring visitors find desert wildflowers. Prickly pear cactus and rattlesnakes are other notable residents.

Canyon Road, as State Highway 821 is known, runs along the east

Beach break on the Yakima River (Dan Hansen photo)

side of the river, which is a mix of private and public land. No houses stand on the opposite shoreline, which includes the L. T. Murray Wildlife Recreation Area and is largely inaccessible by road.

ACCESS

To reach the most popular put-in from Interstate 90, take exit 109 at Ellensburg and drive south on Canyon Road. About 3.5 miles from I-90, turn right onto Ringer Loop Road, and drive another quarter mile to a Washington Fish and Wildlife Department boat launch.

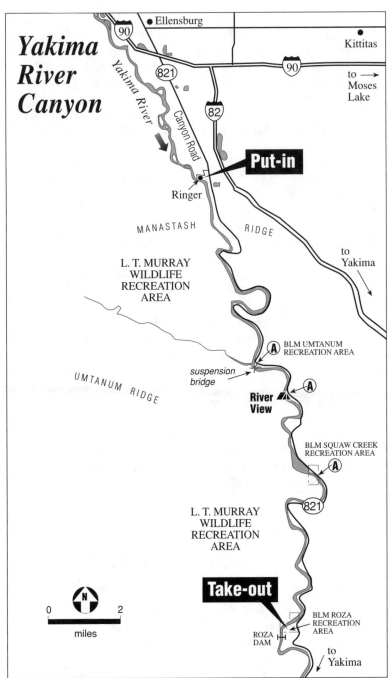

Three U.S. Bureau of Land Management river accesses and a private campground give paddlers an opportunity to customize a trip of anywhere from 9 to 18.5 miles. All accesses are along Canyon Road.

The first access is the BLM Umtanum Recreation Area, 9 miles downstream from Ringer. The take-out is on river-left, just upstream from the suspension footbridge.

The private River View Campground is 10.5 miles downstream from Ringer. The owners charge fees for parking, launching, and camping.

The BLM Squaw Creek and Roza Recreation Areas are 13 and 18.5 miles downstream from Ringer. The Roza access, just upstream from Roza Dam, is the farthest upstream that powerboats are allowed on the Yakima.

PADDLE ROUTE

Flow information	•	USGS Water Resources in Pasco
River gauge	•	12484500 at Umtanum
Historic flows	•	Average 2,416; maximum 41,000; minimum 138

Upstream reservoirs keep the Yakima River high during summer, when farmers need water to grow apples, Timothy hay, and other crops. Although there are no significant rapids, paddlers can count on a swift run with few eddies during the artificially high water. After running bank to bank from April to August, the river drops in fall and winter. These "off-seasons" also bring relief from the powerful winds that plague the canyon in spring, and the heat and party-rafters that bear down on the river in summer. There is no off-season for the trains that rumble through the canyon to wake up campers.

Spring and summer flows at the Umtanum river gauge typically run more than 3,000 cubic feet per second, dropping to an average of 2,100 cfs in September and a little more than 1,000 cfs in November.

7 · Winchester Wasteway

Distance	•	25 miles
Time	•	12 hours or overnight
Season	•	Generally March through mid-October
Shuttle	•	16 miles, pavement
Rating	•	Flatwater

Hazards	•	Two waterfalls, thorn bushes; winds on Potholes Reservoir; hunting
Information	•	Potholes State Park near Othello
Maps	•	USGS Winchester SE, Corfu, Mae, plus Grant County map

Just decades ago, a river did not run through it. The topography was there, carved by post–Ice Age floods. But this stream within the Columbia Basin desert did not emerge in modern times until water was pumped from the Columbia River and spread onto croplands that had been mostly sage and cactus for thousands of years.

Irrigation runoff has been routed into a natural channel en route to Potholes Reservoir, forming one of the most wonderfully obscure paddling adventures in the lower 48 states.

Late winter on Winchester Wasteway (Rich Landers photo)

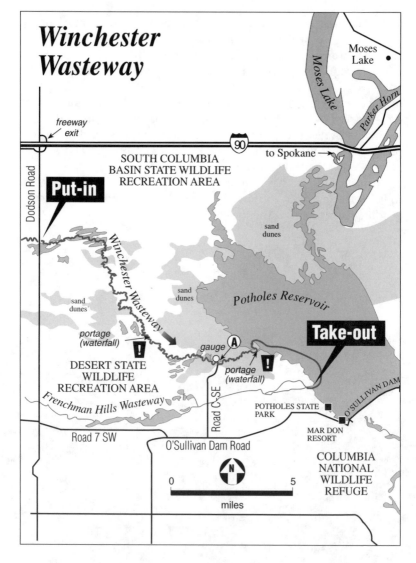

Winchester Wasteway

Spring and early summer are magical times on the wasteway. Nesting waterfowl make a racket that goes on day and night: Then there's the trill of red-winged blackbirds, the clamor of Canada geese, the whine of coyotes, the ratcheting of sandhill cranes.

It's worth making a primitive camp in the sand and sage and

spending the night just to hear the serenade. There's plenty of water for floating, but you'll want to bring drinking water from home. Another option is to paddle down from the put-in and pole or paddle back out in the same day, passing the bullrushes and towering plumes of non-native tall reed grass called *phragmites*. The flow in the section downstream from Dodson Road southwest of Moses Lake is easy to negotiate in either direction.

By late March, paddling conditions can be excellent, although campers can wake to a thick layer of frost on their tents. The leaves have not yet burst from their buds to hide the thorns on the overhanging brush. By April, the vegetation is considerably greener and water is warm enough in the off-channel sloughs to produce good fishing for bass and perch. By June, the grasses begin to turn brown and small potholes dry up in the desert. But the wasteway keeps flowing, boosted by increased irrigation to Columbia Basin crops. Minimum flows ranging from 75 to 90 cubic feet per second generally run from December through mid-April. Runoff events, if any, typically occur from mid-January to mid-February. Maximum flows usually occur from mid-October through early November, ranging from 170 to 190 cfs.

Waterfowl hunters usually close the floating season on the wasteway, setting out decoys along the sloughs in hunts that begin in mid-October.

ACCESS

To reach the put-in from Interstate 90, take the Dodson Road exit about 10 miles west of Moses Lake and head south 3.3 miles to the state-maintained parking site. Paddlers who want to do the through-trip to Potholes Reservoir can make the shuttle by continuing south on Dodson Road. Take the first paved left (east) onto Road 7 SW (Frenchman Hills Road), continuing east on O'Sullivan Dam Road to Potholes State Park.

PADDLE ROUTE

Flow information • Bureau of Reclamation in Ephrata
River gauge • No number
Historic flows • Average 120; maximum 210;
minimum 71

A sense of humor is more useful than a map and compass for navigation in the wasteway. Paddlers may hit dead ends in the dunes and have to backtrack to find the channel. A few miles later, the channel is so narrow and fast you'll be draw-stroking frantically to pivot the canoe into a 90-degree turn. You might have to wade through cattails or duck under branches.

Summer weed growth can obscure the channel in some places. Stir mud with a paddle or watch for weeds bending downstream to track the channel current when the route opens into sloughs or dead-ends against sand dunes. The channel can be shallow in some spots, requiring paddlers to drag canoes briefly over sand.

The wasteway downstream from Dodson Road flows through state-managed land. Sand dunes provide numerous areas for primitive camping. The only notable hazard in the first stretch downstream from Dodson Road is a small waterfall. In some flows, the 2- to 3-foot falls can be run on river-right. The option of an easy portage is on river-left.

Novices—and paddlers who want to keep canoe bottoms pristine—can avoid the tougher section of the wasteway by taking out at the gauging station at roughly the mid-point of this trip. This take-out is accessible from Road C-SE off O'Sullivan Dam Road just west of Potholes State Park.

The lazy nature of the wasteway changes near the gauging station. From here down, paddlers are likely to become acquainted with the thorns of Russian olive trees. The tripper in the bow can avoid them with prayer and a deft draw. The paddler in the stern might put more stock in armor. The channel gets fast and narrow, twisting and rocky in the last leg to Potholes Reservoir.

Downstream from the gauge, on a calm day, paddlers can hear the falls and have a leisurely 100 yards to get out on river-right. On a windy day, first-timers might not detect the falls until they are within 25 or 30 yards. That's still plenty of time if you're not daydreaming.

The water gushes over concrete-like caliche cliffs in a three-stage fall that roars 25 feet down into a deep bowl. The portage around the falls offers its own adventure down a sand dune.

From the falls, a maze of sand dune islands must be negotiated out to Potholes Reservoir. Civilization appears in the form of fishing boats. Head northeast at first, then southeast into the reservoir, skirting the outside of the brushiest dunes toward the tall poplars of Potholes State Park. Only experienced paddlers should attempt this 3-mile open-water stretch in foul weather. The reservoir can be windy, but some protection can be found by snugging up to the lee along the west shore.

8 • Hutchinson and Shiner Lakes

Distance	•	3 miles round trip
Time	•	Variable
Season	•	March through September
Shuttle	•	None
Rating	•	Flatwater
Hazards	•	Wind
Information	•	U.S. Fish and Wildlife Service in Othello
Maps	•	USGS O'Sullivan Dam, plus free Columbia National Wildlife Refuge map

Shiner Lake on Columbia National Wildlife Refuge
(Dan Hansen photo)

The hundreds of lakes and ponds in the Columbia National Wildlife Refuge are an unexpected benefit of Columbia Basin agriculture. Most of the coulees and canyons were dry before irrigation came to the region. Now, the 23,100-acre refuge and surrounding state and private land support uncounted masses of migrating ducks, geese, sandhill cranes, and other birds.

Of all the drive-to waters in the refuge, paddlers find the most solitude on 50-acre Hutchinson Lake and 30-acre Shiner Lake, which are joined by a narrow channel. Special regulations discourage the crowds that mob other nearby lakes each spring and fall. The U.S. Fish and Wildlife Service does not allow hunting, camping, or swimming at Hutchinson and Shiner, which are closed for all uses from October until March. Gasoline-powered boats are prohibited.

The two lakes are not stocked with trout, the most popular gamefish in the region. Fishing can be good for bluegills and bass. The quality of the fishing can vary, depending on the population of carp, which compete with the other species for food and muck up spawning areas. A barrier to prevent carp from entering the lakes was being planned in 1997.

ACCESS

To reach Hutchinson Lake from Othello, Washington, drive north on Broadway Road, past the Nestle potato processing plant and Potholes East Canal. Broadway turns west and becomes McManamon Road at the canal. From there, it's about 7 miles to the well-marked gravel road that leads to Hutchinson Lake, which is a mile off the pavement.

PADDLE ROUTE

From the boat launch on Hutchinson Lake, most paddlers head east on the main lake, then through a narrow passage to Shiner. The channel often is too shallow and weed-choked for bigger boats, but canoes and kayaks normally have little trouble.

Stained basalt walls rise from the lake, broken in places where visitors can leave their boats for a hike through the sage-covered scabland. Watch for cliff swallows that make their nests on the rocks, as well as great horned owls. Rattlesnakes are common in summer.

It's little more than 1.5 miles from the Hutchinson Lake boat launch to the east end of Shiner. Paddlers can easily explore both lakes in the first or last hours of daylight, when wildlife viewing is best. That leaves plenty of time to catch a brace of hatchery trout at one of the more crowded lakes in the refuge, and set up camp where it is permitted.

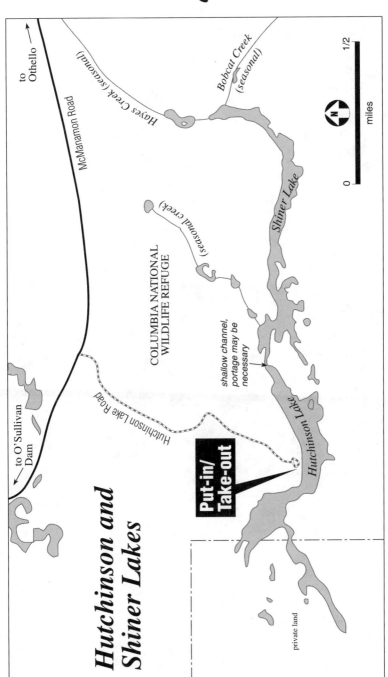

Hutchinson and Shiner Lakes

to Othello →

McManamon Road

Hayes Creek (seasonal)

Bobcat Creek (seasonal)

Shiner Lake

COLUMBIA NATIONAL WILDLIFE REFUGE

(seasonal creek)

shallow channel, portage may be necessary

Hutchinson Lake Road

to O'Sullivan Dam

Put-in/ Take-out

Hutchinson Lake

private land

N

0 1/2 miles

9 · Crab Creek

Distance	•	18 miles
Time	•	10 hours or overnight
Season	•	Virtually year-round
Shuttle	•	17 miles, pavement and gravel
Rating	•	Class 1, with one avoidable Class 2 rapid
Hazards	•	Strong winds, fences, hunting
Information	•	Washington Fish and Wildlife Department in Ephrata
Maps	•	USGS Beverly and Beverly SE

The only significant rapids on lower Crab Creek (Dan Hansen photo)

No matter where one travels in the Columbia Basin, Crab Creek is never far away. Starting as a trickle north of Reardan, the longest creek in Washington winds across three counties before dumping into the Columbia River. In many places, it feeds marshes that are oases for wildlife. To pre-irrigation farmers, the stream meant hope; they built their homes along its banks during rare wet years, assuming it would always provide enough water for their crops and families.

But for all its length—more than 175 miles—Crab Creek lacks staying power in this region where annual rainfall is measured in single digits. In places north of Moses Lake, the creek goes underground. The skeletons of farm houses that were abandoned during drought years are scattered along the banks.

Make no mistake; this is harsh, if fascinating, country. Folks who normally spend their weekends prowling the Northwest's thick forests may feel exposed and vulnerable. When night falls, they'll be stunned by the wide-open view of the stars.

This trip covers Crab Creek's final 18 miles, mostly through land managed by the state Fish and Wildlife Department. It makes a wonderful overnighter for families, with the option of cutting the distance to 7 or 11 miles.

Depending on the season, paddlers will see red-winged and yellow-headed blackbirds, herons, cinnamon teal, and other waterfowl. Birds of prey are common and chukar partridges call from the Saddle Mountains, a stark Ice Age range that stands 1,500 feet above the valley floor. Beavers gnaw on the rare trees and campers can count on a chorus of coyotes to sing them to sleep.

ACCESS

To reach the put-in from Royal City, drive 2 miles east on State Highway 26. Turn south on E. Road SW, and drive about 3 miles to Crab Creek. There is ample parking on the north bank, between the railroad tracks and the road.

To reach the take-out from the put-in, continue south on E. Road SW, which turns west and becomes Lower Crab Creek Road immediately after crossing the creek. At 16 miles, in the town of Beverly, turn left on State Highway 243. Drive a mile to the mouth of Crab Creek, where there's a county park and boat launch on the Columbia River. Theft is a problem at the park; leave nothing valuable in your car.

(For the most direct route to Beverly from Interstate 90, take exit 137 on the east side of the Vantage bridge. Drive south a mile on State Highway 26, then 7 more miles on State Highway 243.)

An alternative access is the bridge where Lower Crab Creek Road crosses the creek. It is 6 road miles east of Beverly.

PADDLE ROUTE

Flow information • USGS Water Resources in Pasco
River gauge • 12465000 near Irby
Historic flows • Average 63; maximum 8,370; minimum 0

Paddlers come to their first, and most dangerous, hazard not more than 20 yards from the put-in, just as they emerge from under the E. Road SW bridge. A barbed-wire fence that spans the creek may offer too little clearance for canoes at high water. Check it out before beginning the trip.

Watch for a second fence with slightly more clearance about 2 miles downstream from the put-in, and a footbridge with extremely low clearance at 5 miles. Other landmarks are an abandoned railroad bridge at 8 miles and a dilapidated wooden bridge that no longer reaches entirely across the creek at 10 miles. The second access is less than a mile downstream from that wooden half-bridge.

For the first 7 miles of this trip, Crab Creek flows slowly, meandering in some places, broadening into marshes in others. Downstream from the railroad bridge it builds speed and narrows.

Below the second access, the creek is swift and narrow, and hemmed between steep banks. It's about 2 miles from the second access to the only significant whitewater, a short Class 2 rapid where the stream rounds a sharp corner and drops over a rock shelf.

No obvious portage goes around the rapid, but a route can be picked along either bank. A large eddy is just downstream.

About a mile below the rapid, the creek widens and slows, passing the Beverly Sand Dunes, a popular playground for motorcyclists and other off-road enthusiasts. (The dunes can serve as an alternate take-out, but only for boaters with four-wheel-drive vehicles.)

The final mile of the stream fluctuates with the Columbia River, creating an ugly, inland tidal flat. Be careful if you step out of the canoe here; the mud is several feet deep in places.

Flows on Crab Creek vary with the weather and irrigation runoff. Since the gauging station is 100 miles upstream, its readings are a poor standard for this trip. Typically, however, spring offers the best combinations of good flows and friendly weather. Summer brings intense heat, along with mosquitoes and the occasional rattlesnake. Winter can leave a crust of ice along the shoreline. Duck hunters use streamside blinds in the fall, but this part of Crab Creek is too muddy for

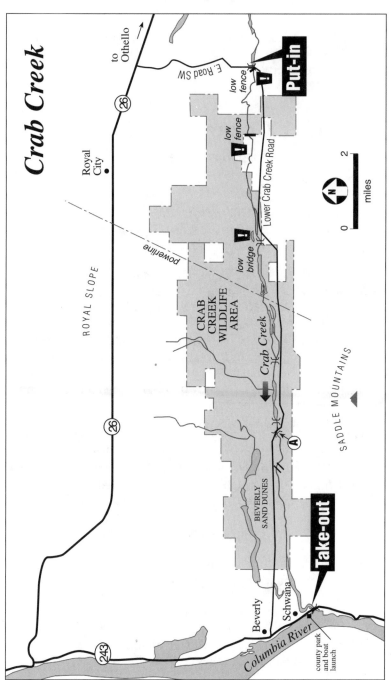

Crab Creek

good fishing, so it is virtually unused the rest of the year.

Paddlers should be aware that westerly winds strong enough to push a boat upstream can hit during any season. They are most prevalent in the late afternoon and evening.

10 · Columbia River
(Hanford Reach)

Distance •	33 miles
Time •	2 days
Season •	Virtually year-round
Shuttle •	25.5 miles first day, 35 miles second day, pavement and gravel
Rating •	Class 1–2
Hazards •	Strong winds; powerful eddies, boils
Information •	U.S. Fish and Wildlife Service in Othello; Washington Fish and Wildlife Department in Ephrata
Maps •	USGS Vernita, Coyote Rapids, Locke Island, Hanford, Savage Island, plus Benton, Grant, and Franklin County maps

For all practical purposes, this is two trips, not one, on the last major free-flowing stretch of the Columbia (see trip 24 for another Columbia River trip). While the nuclear plants that line the western shoreline of Hanford Reach no longer operate, the Department of Energy keeps things under tight wraps. The public is allowed to go ashore only in the Wahluke Wildlife Area, and then only during daylight hours. Camping or overnight parking is prohibited. A boat-in campsite at the White Bluffs access has been proposed.

The trip involves 18 miles of paddling the first day and 15 miles the second. While there are no rapids, paddlers should be cautious of strong eddies and crosscurrents. The size and remoteness of the river means a spill could be fatal. Strong winds can develop suddenly, and summer brings intense heat. Paddlers should carry plenty of water.

ACCESS

To reach the put-in from Interstate 90, take exit 137 on the east side of the Columbia near the Vantage bridge. Drive south a mile on State Highway 26, then 28 miles on State Highway 243. The access, used mostly by anglers, is a rough track through the sagebrush to the river's edge, just upstream from the Vernita bridge. Vehicles with low clearance might scrape rocks.

To reach the middle access, drive east from the Vernita bridge 19 miles on State Highway 24. Just past milepost 63, turn right at the entrance to the Wahluke Wildlife Area. Follow the access road, which alternates between gravel and very rough pavement, about 4 miles to the only significant crossroads. Turn right and drive another 1.5 miles to the White Bluffs access. Overnight parking has not been allowed as of 1997. The state Fish and Wildlife Department sometimes closes this access in winter and spring to protect waterfowl. Check with the agency's Ephrata office.

The take-out is near the Ringold fish hatchery. From the middle access, continue east another 10 miles on Highway 24, turning right

Columbia River near White Bluffs (Julie Titone photo)

on Sagehill Road, near milepost 74. At 11 miles, Sagehill comes to a T with Road 170. Turn right again, driving about 4 miles to a Y in the road. Stay right, on what is now Rickert Road. At 2 miles, cross Ringold River Road and follow a rough dirt road a few hundred feet to the river.

To reach the Ringold take-out, from U.S. Highway 395, drive west on State Highway 17 about 2 miles, through the town of Mesa. Turn left on Road 170 and drive 9 miles to the junction with Sagehill Road. From that point, follow the above directions.

PADDLE ROUTE

Flow information • USGS Water Resources in Pasco
River gauge • 12472800 below Priest Rapids Dam
Historic flows • Average 118,000; maximum 693,000;
minimum 4,120

Ignore the ominous nuclear reactors to the west (where cleanup will continue for decades and trespassing is a federal offense), and Hanford Reach looks little different than it did when European settlers first arrived. Few other trips in the Inland Northwest offer better wildlife viewing. Eagles and hawks ride the air currents created by 400-foot cliffs known as the White Bluffs. White pelicans—a species listed as endangered in Washington State—drift over the river. The Reach's 17 islands are predator-safe fawning grounds for mule deer in the spring and a sanctuary for 70,000 ducks and geese in late fall and early winter.

The Reach supports about 90 percent of the wild fall chinook salmon that still spawn in the Columbia. They draw scores of anglers in all manner of powerboats in autumn. Anglers also find healthy numbers of giant sturgeon, one of the oldest species on earth. This is the last toehold for the Columbia River limpet and the Columbia pebblesnail. Biologists still are discovering new species of plants and insects on the land surrounding the Reach.

The White Bluffs are rich in fossils, including bones of extinct bison, horses, and mastodon. Remains of a blacksmith's shop still stand near the White Bluffs access, where the military camped during the Yakama Indian War (1855–1858). The access was a ferry crossing until the government ordered residents to move from the area so it could begin weapons production in secret. Farther downstream on the western shore, the Hanford school has stood empty since the 1940s.

Even in areas where public access is allowed, it is illegal to disturb fossils, artifacts, or the remains of buildings.

Discharges from Priest Rapids Dam can significantly alter flow in the Reach during a day.

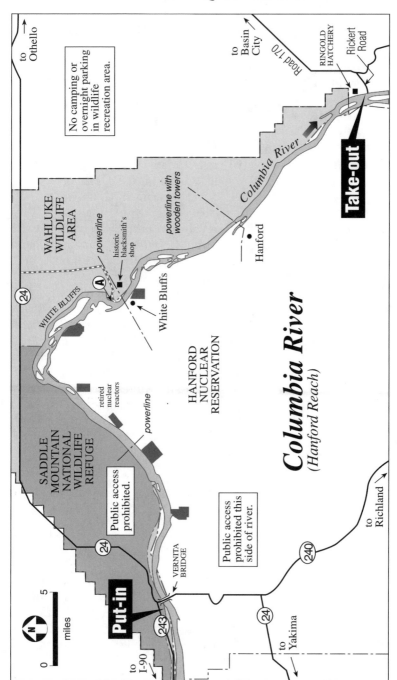

Columbia River
(Hanford Reach)

11 • Walla Walla River

Distance	•	4 miles
Time	•	1 hour
Season	•	March through September
Shuttle	•	5 miles, pavement and gravel
Rating	•	Flatwater
Hazards	•	Wind
Information	•	McNary Dam in Umatillo, Oregon
Maps	•	USGS Wallula, Zangar Junction, plus free Wallula Habitat Management Unit map

The casual observer may miss the beauty in the final miles of the Walla Walla River. Its banks are steep and muddy, its backwaters shallow and uninviting. The river is sluggish from the effects of McNary Dam on the Columbia River and stained brown from the farm runoff. It does not support trout, although steelhead run upstream in winter. Instead, transplanted channel catfish prowl the depths while big carp splash in the cattails. Even the put-in is difficult.

Yet there is beauty in the river bottom, which stands as a lush ribbon in an otherwise drab landscape. The U.S. Army Corps of Engineers plants wheat on either side of the river to attract wildlife. In spring and summer, paddlers may see flocks of nesting American avocets and migrating pelicans. In fall and winter, the valley is alive with ducks and geese, and is a popular spot for bird hunters. The Walla Walla begins in the Blue Mountains at the confluence of the North Fork and South Fork and runs 50 miles to the Columbia. Camping is available at Madame Dorion Memorial Park near the take-out.

ACCESS

To reach the take-out, drive 17 miles south from Pasco on U.S. Highway 12. Just south of the Walla Walla River, veer left at the Y known as Wallula Junction, then immediately take another left into a roadside picnic area. A rough dirt road leads from the picnic grounds to the river.

To reach the put-in, drive east on Highway 12 from Wallula Junction. Turn left on Game Department Road, about 3 miles from the junction. From October through February the road is gated and locked a half mile from the highway. Paddlers must carry their canoes another half mile to the river. If the gate is open, drive to the river, then turn right and drive another half mile upstream, launching at any of several openings anglers have cleared through the riverside brush. The

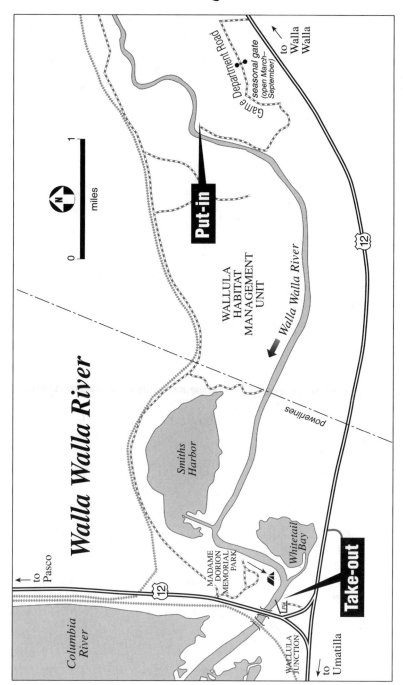

Walla Walla River

bank is slick with mud, and stepping from the steep shoreline into a canoe can be tricky.

PADDLE ROUTE

Flow information • USGS Water Resources in Pasco
River gauge • 14018500 at Touchet
Historic flows • Average 559; maximum 20,300; minimum 0

Once on the water, there are few hazards to upset a canoe or kayak. The Walla Walla is broad and deep, and the current is nearly imperceptible. Paddlers may wish to explore either of two ponds linked to the river by narrow sloughs.

12 • Palouse Falls

Distance • 13 miles round trip
Time • 5–8 hours
Season • Generally late February through May
Shuttle • None
Rating • Class 2, with upstream paddling
Hazards • Portaging or tracking canoes upstream through rapids over rocky, brushy shoreline; rattlesnakes, poison ivy; turbulence at base of falls
Information • Lyons Ferry State Park near Starbuck
Maps • USGS Palouse Falls, Starbuck West

Even amenable paddlers can find good reason on this trip to go against the flow. The lower Palouse River offers a mix of flatwater and running water leading into one of the region's most spectacular canoeable gorges. Basalt cliffs gradually close in on the river until paddlers reach the stunning amphitheater of Palouse Falls. The reward is paddling into the pool and looking up 198 feet to where the huge column of water plunges off the rimrock.

Careful canoeists can frolic in the spray, but there is never enough room to paddle safely behind the falls. Indeed, in high spring flows, the falls create big waves, wind, and a vortex that wants to draw boats into the deathtrap. Enjoy this powerful sight from a safe distance.

The stretch of river upstream from the falls to Hooper rates up to Class 4 in a dangerous gauntlet of vertical basalt walls that makes it difficult to bail out. Even this tamer lower river has challenges between the falls and the start near the Snake River at Lyons Ferry State Park. Going upstream, paddlers will have to use ropes to track their boats in several sections. Poison ivy lines the banks in places upstream, and rattlesnakes are always a possibility. On the return trip, expect three rapids ranging to Class 2.

ACCESS

The trip begins and ends in Lyons Ferry State Park at the confluence of the Palouse and Snake Rivers. The park is between the small Washington towns of Washtucna and Starbuck on State Highway 261. The entrance to the park is at the north end of the highway bridge over

Lower Palouse River canyon, en route to Palouse Falls
(Rich Landers photo)

the Snake River. Follow signs to the boat launch area and a fine spread of green grass, usually well sprinkled with wild goose droppings. Also from near the park entrance, a gravel road leads a little farther north to a primitive launch for small boats near the old ferry exhibit. This launch doesn't have grass, but it saves boaters the effort of paddling out and around a large breakwater.

PADDLE ROUTE

Flow information • USGS Water Resources in Spokane
River gauge • 13351000 at Hooper
Historic flows • Average 582; maximum 35,500; minimum 0

The pool backed up 28 miles on the Snake behind Lower Monumental Dam floods the basin at the mouth of the Palouse, making it broad like a lake. The first 3 miles up the Palouse are slackwater suitable for novice paddlers and powerboats. Most paddlers with some experience can handle current that gradually builds in a transition zone. The exact end of the slackwater depends on Palouse flows and the level of the Snake.

Shortly after the put-in, paddlers will come to the Marmes (pronounced MAR-mus) rock shelter, an archeological site discovered in 1962. In 1968, Washington State University scientists unearthed an ancient skeleton dating back 10,000 years—the oldest human remains discovered at that time in the Western Hemisphere. Unfortunately, the find came one year before the site was to be flooded by Lower Monumental Dam. Progress was not about to be stopped, but the U.S. Army Corps of Engineers agreed to build a dike around the entrance to the cave as a last-ditch effort to preserve the dig site. The dike leaked. Water seeped in, and the cave, one of the world's great archeological finds, is flooded by what is now called Marmes Pond. "Marmes" is the name of the ranch family who once owned land at the shelter site. A mudbar extends out from the dike. Powerboaters give it a wide berth as they head up the Palouse to fish for bass, crappies, and catfish.

The ideal flow for doing the entire trip is roughly 550 cubic feet per second measured upstream at Hooper. However, the upstream trip is still reasonable up to nearly 2,000 cfs. Low flows make it virtually impossible to avoid rocks in rapids. High flows make upstream paddling more difficult and leave less room along the shore to track canoes around rapids. Some tracking is required regardless of flows. Bring long lines for both the bow and stern.

Once at the pool below the falls, canoeists can paddle into the

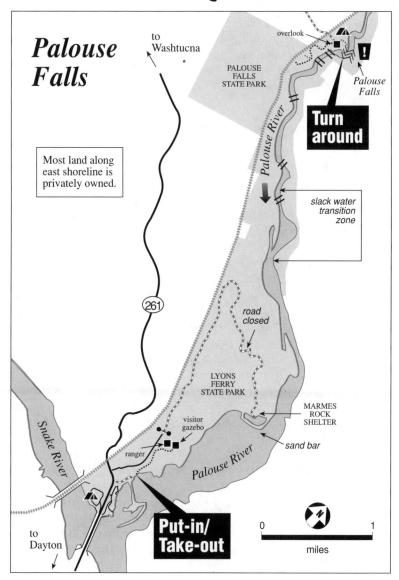

Palouse Falls

to Washtucna

PALOUSE FALLS STATE PARK

overlook

Palouse River

Palouse Falls

Turn around

Most land along east shoreline is privately owned.

slack water transition zone

(261)

road closed

LYONS FERRY STATE PARK

MARMES ROCK SHELTER

visitor gazebo

ranger

sand bar

Palouse River

Snake River

Put-in/ Take-out

to Dayton

0 1
miles

pool and picnic in the basin. Just be careful.

In late April and early May, wildflowers such as arrowleaf balsamroot, lupine, and wild hyacinth bloom along the shore. This coincides with prime time for paddling—and the peak of the tick season. State park rules prohibit firearms, random camping, and camp-fires. A small campground is available at the Palouse Falls State Park overlook. A larger campground overlooks the Snake River at Lyons Ferry, the headquarters for both state parks. Both parks feature short hiking trails.

13 • Palouse River

Distance	•	16 miles
Time	•	5 hours
Season	•	Generally March and April
Shuttle	•	6 miles, pavement and gravel
Rating	•	Class 1-plus
Hazards	•	Strainers, debris, sharp rocks
Information	•	National Resources Conservation Service in Colfax
Maps	•	USGS Palouse, Elberton

For most of the year from the U.S. Highway 195 bridge in Colfax, Washington, all you see is a skim of water beneath 20-foot concrete walls. The Palouse River doesn't look appealing to paddlers in a region with so many spectacular options. But the flood control channels are a clue that the Palouse isn't always a trickle. During the brief weeks of high water, knowledgeable paddlers head to the canyons up and down-stream from Colfax, where the walls are basalt, rather than concrete, and the Palouse is still a river.

From its source in the Hoodoo Mountains of the St. Joe National Forest, the Palouse gathers from a tangle of small tributaries. When water conditions are right, the stream is floatable for about 120 miles from Laird Park Campground east of Harvard, Idaho, to the confluence with the Snake River. In that length, the river ranges to Class 4 in some stretches, with obvious portages around the flood control chan-nels at Colfax and at the dangerous gorge upstream from Palouse Falls (see trip 12).

This trip covers a manageable 16 miles. It starts in the small town of Palouse, Washington, and ends in Elberton, which is little more than a ghost town. There is one alternative access, at Eden Valley, to cut the trip in half.

Palouse River near Elberton (Rich Landers photo)

ACCESS

To reach the Palouse put-in, follow State Highway 272 east from Colfax for 17 miles. Turn right on Division Street and right again on Main Street, which leads in about a quarter of a mile to the city park. There is plenty of room for parking and launching boats at the park.

To reach the Eden Valley access (which can serve as take-out for the upper section or put-in for the lower stretch), turn north off Highway 272 on Altergott Road. The gravel road is about 4 miles west of Palouse, and just west of milepost 8. Altergott crosses the river less than a mile from the highway.

The Elberton take-out is reached via Brown Road, which stems off Highway 272 about 10 miles east of Colfax (7 miles west of Palouse). Drive north on this gravel road 3.5 miles to its intersection with Oral Smith Road, which immediately crosses the river.

Paddlers coming from the Spokane area can shave several miles off the trip to Elberton by turning east off U.S. Highway 195 at Dry Creek Road (the Garfield exit) just south of Steptoe. Drive 3 miles to Elberton Road, which is gravel, then another 3 miles over the Palouse River and through Elberton, to Oral Smith Road and the put-in.

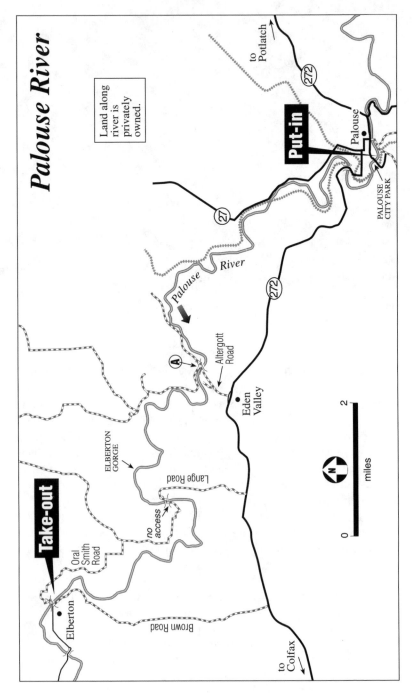

Palouse River

Land along river is privately owned.

PADDLE ROUTE

Flow information • USGS Water Resources in Spokane
River gauge • 13351000 at Hooper
Historic flows • Average 582; maximum 35,500; minimum 0

People accustomed to the region's rolling hills will be surprised at this river trip. Basalt walls rise 200 feet in places. Elsewhere, the river flows through open pine and fir forests.

Paddlers can see a variety of waterfowl and birds of prey. Broken shells provide evidence that freshwater mussels still survive in the muddy Palouse. River otters live here, too, perhaps drawn by the mussels. Sportsmen introduced Rio Grande turkeys to the region in the 1970s.

Timing is key. The most scenic portion of this trip—8 miles from Eden Valley to Elberton—is best experienced when water is flowing at roughly 800 to 1,700 cubic feet per second. That window of opportunity typically comes during warm spells in March. At lower flows, paddlers must walk through long stretches, and canoes constantly scrape sharp rocks.

The upper 8 miles, from Palouse to Eden Valley, has a longer season and calmer water, but is cluttered with unsightly debris, including junk cars used to shore up denuded riverbanks. Some of the cars washed into the channel during the floods of 1996, giving paddlers the rare opportunity to perform eddy turns behind Fords and Buicks. Although less scenic than the lower stretch, this is a good option for beginning paddlers, and can be run at flows as low as 400 cfs.

In 1995, the U.S. Geological Survey stopped recording river flows at Colfax, leaving paddlers to rely on the Hooper gauge, many miles downstream. Some guesswork is involved since readings at Hooper can be skewed by heavy flows on the South Fork of the Palouse. Generally, however, the flow at Elberton is half what it is at Hooper.

14 • Bonnie Lake

Distance • 11 miles round trip
Time • Half day or overnight
Season • March through October
Shuttle • None
Rating • Flatwater

Hazards	•	Wind
Information	•	Bureau of Land Management in Spokane
Maps	•	USGS Chapman Lake, Pine City, plus Spokane and Whitman County maps

Bonnie Lake isn't convenient. The 600-foot cliffs that surround it are known only to a few farmers, anglers, and canoeists. It can't be seen from any road, but is reached by paddling almost a mile up a sluggish

Paddling down Rock Creek from Bonnie Lake (Rich Landers photo)

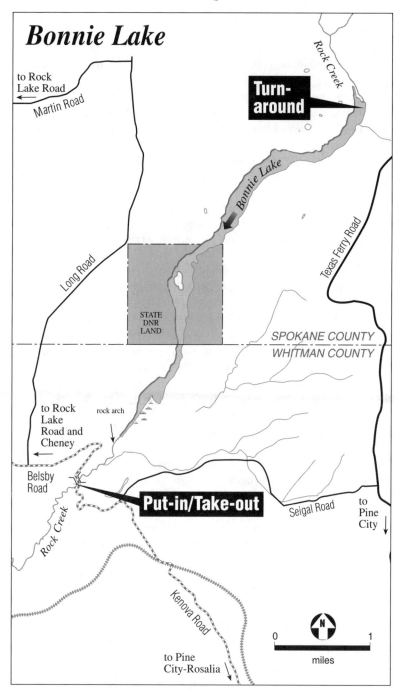

Bonnie Lake

to Rock Lake Road
Martin Road

Rock Creek

Turn-around

Bonnie Lake

Long Road

Texas Ferry Road

STATE DNR LAND

SPOKANE COUNTY
WHITMAN COUNTY

to Rock Lake Road and Cheney

rock arch

Belsby Road

Put-in/Take-out

Rock Creek

Seigal Road

to Pine City

Kenova Road

to Pine City-Rosalia

0   1
N
miles

creek that is nearly dry by August. Only canoes, rafts, and car-top boats with small motors can make the trip, so the lake is a fairly quiet get-away, an hour from Spokane.

Bonnie Lake is home to red-tailed hawks and turkey vultures in the summer, and bald eagles and a variety of waterfowl in the fall and spring. Raccoons feed on the lake's crayfish, as do bass, perch, and crappie. Keep your ears tuned for the cascading song of canyon wrens and the flurry of red-winged and yellow-headed blackbirds. This is rattlesnake country.

Be aware that strong winds are nearly a certainty in the afternoon. Few bays offer security in big blows, and vertical rock shorelines in some areas make beaching impossible. An easy 1- or 2-hour up-lake paddle could possibly turn into an epic on the return trip. Be patient.

Boaters must carry drinking water from home, since Bonnie Lake is a catch basin for runoff from surrounding farms and ranches.

ACCESS

To reach the lake from the south end of Cheney, drive just over 17 miles south on Cheney-Plaza Road, the route to Turnbull National Wildlife Refuge. (Past Turnbull, the road becomes Rock Lake Road.) Turn left (east) on Miller Road, which becomes Belsby Road. In 4 miles, this gravel road starts dropping into Hole-in-the-Ground, as the dramatic canyon between Bonnie and Rock Lakes is known. At nearly 5 miles, the road crosses Rock Creek. The put-in is on the southwest side of the bridge, and the lake is out of sight to the northeast. Park as far off the road as possible so farmers can pass with combines and trailers.

From the south, Bonnie Lake can be reached by taking Malden Road from Rosalia. A half-mile past Pine City, turn right onto Stephen Road. After a mile, take another right onto Hole In The Ground Road, the second of twin dirt roads. It is 4 miles from this junction to the Rock Creek bridge.

PADDLE ROUTE

Canoeists paddling up the narrow creek (the current is negligible) may wonder why they bother. Cattails, water lilies, and canary grass hem in the stagnant waterway, and the creek bottom is thick with mud. Cattle—and, sometimes, domestic bison—can startle boaters as they peer down from banks that rise 2 feet above the creek. Snakes, muskrats, and other creatures slip into the cattails as boaters pass. A half mile upstream, visitors can see a rock arch high on the northwest cliff. Geologists believe the canyon, and the arch, were formed by floods at the end of the last Ice Age. This natural bridge apparently was hollowed out of a basalt wall by glacial flood eddies.

The cramped creek eventually opens into Bonnie Lake, which appears smaller than it is. Four miles long and a half mile wide, the lake fills the canyon, following the contours of cliffs. Only short stretches of the lake are visible at any time. Cliff swallows swarm at a canoeist's eye level, as they fly down from their nests in several basalt walls. Although the land surrounding the lake is privately owned, an island a third of the way uplake is public land co-managed by the U.S. Bureau of Land Management and state Department of Natural Resources. It's a good place to camp, but this is no place for campfires. The evidence is in the charred ponderosa pines that stud the island. This area gets very dry beginning in late spring.

15 • Fishtrap Lake

Distance	•	8 miles round trip
Time	•	3 hours
Season	•	Generally March through October
Shuttle	•	None
Rating	•	Flatwater
Hazards	•	Wind
Information	•	Bureau of Land Management in Spokane; Fishtrap Lake Resort
Maps	•	USGS Fishtrap Lake, plus BLM Fishtrap-Miller Ranch map sheet one

In less than an hour from the congestion of Spokane, a paddler can be plying the quiet waters of Fishtrap Lake. Blaring horns and cursing drivers are replaced by soaring raptors, songbirds, and waterfowl. Basalt cliffs take the place of office walls.

Just make sure it's not opening week of fishing season in late April, when congestion at the lake will be worse than it was downtown. Better to visit Fishtrap Lake in the quiet days before the opener, when the scattered aspens are just starting to wake to spring. Or wait until late May, when most anglers have given up the chase for hatchery-raised trout. Powerboats are common on the lake, but since water skiing is prohibited, there is little reason for boaters to travel fast.

Entering The Narrows at Fishtrap Lake (Rich Landers photo)

ACCESS

To reach the lake, take exit 254 from Interstate 90 (about 27 miles west of Spokane) and drive south 2.5 miles. Turn left on Scroggie Road, which leads to the Fishtrap Lake Resort and a public boat launch on the north end of the lake.

PADDLE ROUTE

The resort and a cluster of cabins and trailers that surrounds it are the only development on the lake. Yet the area has a colorful recreation history documented from 1900, when an area trapper established a rustic fishing resort with a few rowboats at the inlet, where Hog Canyon Creek flows into this basalt-rimmed lake.

In the early days, the resort workers would run a team of horses pulling a livery wagon up the road to the Northern Pacific railroad

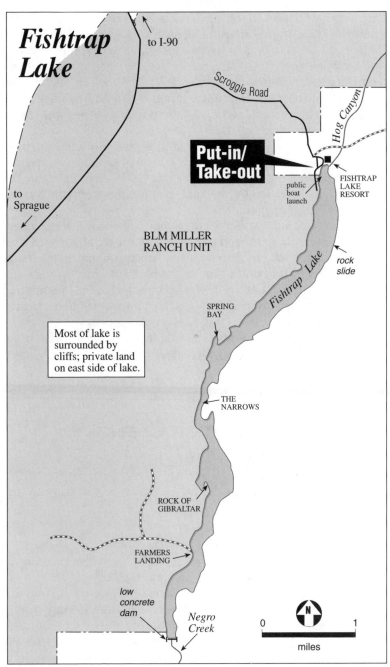

Fishtrap
Lake

to I-90

Scroggie Road

Hog Canyon

FISHTRAP
LAKE RESORT

**Put-in/
Take-out**

public
boat
launch

to Sprague

BLM MILLER
RANCH UNIT

Fishtrap Lake

rock
slide

SPRING
BAY

Most of lake is
surrounded by
cliffs; private land
on east side of lake.

THE
NARROWS

ROCK OF
GIBRALTAR

FARMERS
LANDING

low
concrete
dam

Negro
Creek

N

0   1

miles

stop four days a week to shuttle campers who came from throughout the area to fish. The resort's stone house and hotel were built between 1910 and 1912. The large wooden dance hall that straddles the inlet was built just after World War I, becoming the gathering spot for lively Fourth of July celebrations. But the depression took its toll, and the resort fell into disrepair. World War II hurt business further. The once-elegant hall in its scenic setting has been used as little more than a boathouse ever since.

Cliffs along the rest of the lake limit access. One farmer, Charles Miller, sold his 8,000 acres to the U.S. Bureau of Land Management in 1992, preserving the west side of the lake against development. The land, with its 3,500 acres of wetlands and hundreds of potholes, had been in Miller's family since 1871.

Boaters who want to explore the public land can beach at Farmer's Landing, near the south end of the lake. A rough, abandoned road leads through open pine forests to the sagebrush-bunchgrass range above. Hikers might catch a glimpse of a bluebird, coyote, turkey vulture, or mule deer. Camping is allowed only with a BLM permit that must be secured in advance. Campers must pitch their tents at least a quarter mile from the lake. Campfires are prohibited.

Fishtrap Lake and the adjacent BLM land are popular with hunters from mid-October through December.

16 • Hangman Creek
(Latah Creek)

Distance	•	11 miles
Time	•	3–4 hours
Season	•	Generally January through April
Shuttle	•	8 miles, pavement
Rating	•	Class 1, some Class 2
Hazards	•	Blowdown trees; rocks in low water; two points of possible Class 2-plus rapids
Information	•	USGS Water Resources in Spokane
Maps	•	USGS Spokane SW, plus Spokane County map

Hangman Creek is the delight of opportunists, the bane of procrastinators. Most of the year, especially in summer, the flows are too low for paddling. The exceptions are during mid-winter thaws, late-winter runoff, and the occasional soaking rainstorm of summer and fall. Flows sufficient for paddling can develop in hours, and disappear nearly as fast. In these brief moments of opportunity, the creek is a standout paddle trip, complete with scenic rock and sand cliffs, wildlife, and playful rapids.

The official name for the creek is either Hangman or Latah, depending on which official source you cite. Hangman Creek became the common name after the military hanged several tribal leaders along the shores in 1858. (See pages 44–45.)

Hangman Creek begins in the St. Joe National Forest and flows roughly 70 miles through farm valleys from southeast of Tensed, Idaho, through Tekoa, Washington, to the confluence with the Spokane River. From the forest, it flows in a fecund ribbon of rock and greenery

Sand cliffs near Qualchan Golf Course on Hangman Creek (Rich Landers photo)

through Eastern Washington wheat country. Even where the creek wanders near the south edge of Spokane, it is an exceptional wildlife area. Paddlers will find sand beaches in lower flows. Wildlife includes beavers, muskrats, great blue herons and other waterfowl, white-tailed deer, and hawks.

The upper sections of the river are rarely floatable. However, rafters and kayakers rush to run big flushes that create Class 3 and even Class 4 rapids in the canyon east of Spangle.

ACCESS

From Interstate 90 west of Spokane, drive 5 miles south on U.S. Highway 195. Turn left onto Hatch Road. Cross the bridge over Hangman Creek and note the optional river access along the bridge on the upstream side. Continue a short way and turn right on Hangman Valley Road. Drive 2.5 miles to a small turnout on the creek side of the road. (Look across the creek for an old farm house that was demolished by a toppled ponderosa pine.) Do not block the private dirt road that leads closer to the water unless you have permission from the landowners. There is room enough for two cars to park by the road at this undeveloped put-in. Boats can be lowered directly off the road right-of-way to the water. Some boaters rate this a Class 2 paddle trip with a Class 3 put-in.

To reach the take-out, from the junction with Hatch Road, head north on Highway 195 for 4.3 miles and turn left (west) onto 16th Avenue (this is the last center turn lane before reaching I-90). The road bends north and becomes Lindeke. At the first stoplight, drive straight across Sunset Boulevard onto Government Way. Drive 1.3 miles and make a sharp right onto Riverside Avenue. Go a short way and cross the bridge over Hangman Creek. Parking is available upstream and downstream of the bridge. The take-out is on the downstream side of the bridge, river-right.

PADDLE ROUTE

Flow information	• USGS Water Resources in Spokane
River gauge	• 1242400 at Spokane
Historic flows	• Average 266; maximum 20,600; minimum 1

Gauging whether Hangman Creek is floatable can be tricky for the uninitiated. Half of the watershed is crop land. Gone are most of the forests, wetlands, and grass prairies that once filtered runoff, stored groundwater, and rationed flows into the creek through the year.

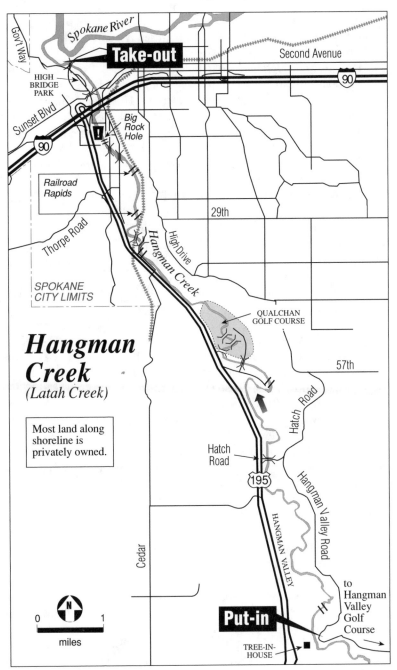

Hangman Creek

Technically, flows above 1,200 cubic feet per second are preferable to avoid banging on rocks in numerous riffles. Visually, if the creek is running fairly clear, it's too low to float.

For another rough gauge of whether this trip will leave the bottom of your boat unscathed, go to the Riverside Avenue bridge at the take-out. Look at the bridge abutment on river-left. The river should be high enough to cover the concrete ledge at the base of the abutment.

The creek is susceptible to flooding that can alter the channel, form logjams, and drop trees into the water. The numerous riffles in this stretch are not a factor at adequate flows, but are definite boat denters in low flows.

The stretch from the put-in to Hatch Road includes only one significant rapid, which can rate up to Class 2 in high flows. The first major skill test comes after a placid pool leads to a sharp left turn upstream from Qualchan Golf Course and behind a subdivision. The short, rocky drop of Bridlewood Rapid can bounce boats in lower water. Large standing waves can swamp boats in high or low water. Scout the rapid. Homeowners may be sitting on their decks to witness your mistakes.

Several bridges through Qualchan Golf Course pose little problem to alert paddlers, as long as logs or debris are not piled up and blocking the channel. Then the river braids into flats. Expect to bounce or step out of the canoe here in flows of less than 1,200 cfs. Pass under steep, captivating sand cliffs with shallow caves carved by high water that scours out large chunks of rock.

After flowing along Highway 195, the creek makes a hard right turn at a railroad bridge (with a standing wave that can be avoided) followed by a hard left turn that can be tricky for some paddlers. From here, boaters will see the effect of man's hand in straightening Hangman Creek for flood control in the early 1930s. The channel becomes deeper, narrower, and boulder-strewn. The flows increase through a long stretch known as Railroad Rapids.

Perhaps the most notable obstacle is Big Rock Hole, a large midstream obstacle just past the Chestnut Street bridge. The big rock forms a challenging standing wave, and a hole at certain flows. Scouting is recommended.

The last stretch of the trip flows under the elegant arches of the old Sunset Highway bridge, past Spokane's rustic High Bridge Park to the take-out. If you were to proceed a short way beyond the take-out, you'd reach the Spokane River (see trip 19). In summer, when Hangman Creek is too low to paddle, there is a large beach at the confluence. Beach patrons do not always wear swimsuits.

In the last half of the twentieth century, the lower reaches of the stream have been virtually void of sportfish. But sportsmen, landowners, and government agencies were beginning to work together in the 1990s to slowly rehabilitate the Hangman watershed, offering hope that the creek flows might someday be accommodating even to procrastinating paddlers.

SPOKANE RIVER SEGMENTS

Trips 17, 18, and 19 take paddlers down particular portions of the Spokane River. For perspective, here is an overview of the river's popular paddling stretches:

- *Post Falls to Harvard Road*—Splashy Class 1 rapids, strong eddies. (See trip 17.)
- *Harvard Road to Plantes Ferry Park*—Class 2 rapids with play holes, the most popular stretch for canoeists and kayakers. (See trip 18.)
- *Plantes Ferry Park to Upriver Dam*—Starts with riffles through boulders, then enters slack water behind Upriver Dam near Donkey Island. Flatwater continues to dam.
- *Upriver Dam to Division Street*—Interesting Class 1 paddling, but no formal put-in or take-out available.
- *Division Street to Monroe Street*—Closed to boating. This section includes Riverfront Park and the deadly Spokane Falls.
- *Maple Street to Meenach Bridge*—Class 1-plus water. (See trip 19.)
- *Meenach Bridge to Seven Mile Bridge*—Includes difficult rapids that range from Class 3 to Class 4 in some flow conditions. Recommended only for expert rafters and paddlers. Take-out is at Plese Flat on river-right upstream from Seven Mile Bridge.

17 · Spokane River
(Corbin Park to Harvard Road)

Distance	•	7 miles
Time	•	2 hours
Season	•	Virtually year-round
Shuttle	•	7.5 miles, pavement
Rating	•	Class 1-plus
Hazards	•	Bridge abutments; powerful eddies and turbulence in high water; boulders and strong eddylines in low water

Information • Spokane County Sheriff marine deputies
Maps • USGS Post Falls, Liberty Lake

Paddlers looking for a wilderness experience won't find it on the upper Spokane River. Scores of floaters on everything from inner tubes to driftboats dot the water on some days during summer. The Centennial Trail brings a parade of walkers, skaters, anglers, and bicyclists to the river's banks. Yet there is a wildness about this stretch that serves as a natural attraction for Post Falls, Idaho, and the city of Spokane.

The 16 miles of river from below Post Falls Dam to the beginning of slackwater behind Upriver Dam flows through a setting of suburbs and industry. Yet most of the south riverbank within Washington is protected from development by the Centennial Trail corridor, which is managed by Riverside State Park and Spokane County. The shoreline above the high water mark in Idaho is privately owned.

Serviceberry and mock orange bloom on the shores in spring, creating walls of white accented with the yellow of arrowleaf balsamroot. This wild habitat attracts quail, rabbits, and other creatures. Once or twice a year, someone reports seeing a cougar, bear, bobcat, or moose that has wandered down to the river, possibly from as far away as Mount Spokane. Ospreys are a common sight over the river, which provides rainbow and brown trout for both the birds and anglers.

The beauty of the Spokane River for Spokane–Coeur d'Alene area residents is that it can be sampled a section at a time, even on a whim after work. This section is choice for paddlers who want splashy riffles and possible play areas, but no unavoidable boat-swamping challenges.

Paddlers heading out to do this interstate trip should be prepared to comply with various rules. In the late 1990s, for example, Idaho's Kootenai County required any small craft to carry a whistle or horn for emergency signaling. Idaho also required all vessels to carry life vests for each person aboard. In Washington, however, Spokane County required everyone floating the Spokane River to *wear* a life vest.

ACCESS

To reach the put-in from Interstate 90, take the Pleasant View Road exit 2 at the west edge of Post Falls. Go south to the stoplight and turn left (east) on Railroad Avenue. Go half a mile and turn right (south) onto Corbin Road, which winds down to the park along the shore of the river.

Travel to the take-out requires backtracking to I-90 and heading west toward Spokane. Take the Liberty Lake exit 296. At the intersection, turn north on Harvard Road. Cross the Spokane River bridge and immediately turn left into the access site.

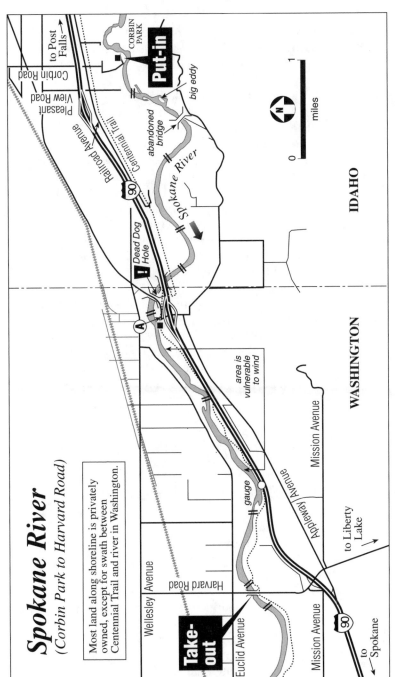

Spokane River
(Corbin Park to Harvard Road)

Most land along shoreline is privately owned, except for swath between Centennial Trail and river in Washington.

PADDLE ROUTE

Flow information	• Avista Utilities recording at Post Falls Dam
Historic flows	• Average 6,139; maximum 49,800; minimum 67

From the calm waters at Corbin Park, boaters soon get their first taste of splashy water. Rapids and eddylines for a mile below the put-in are as difficult as any found en route to Harvard Road. Use common sense in avoiding hazards posed by bridge abutments. Expect turbulence around big pilings at the I-90 bridge. Skilled kayakers like to play in Dead Dog Hole, created by a rock outcrop under the old state line highway bridge at river-right just downstream from I-90.

Soon after passing under the I-90 bridge there is an optional take-out at the Centennial Trail access behind the state line highway weigh station on river-left. This is accessible from I-90's Stateline exit 299.

The river is tame from here to Harvard Road. However, boulders can be hard to avoid in low flows of late summer. Also, a headwind can slow your progress in more than a mile of straight stretches downstream from the state line. Be prepared for the eddy at the take-out just after passing under the Harvard bridge.

In spring flows of 19,000 cubic feet per second, paddlers can do this route in an hour. More typical summer flows under 3,000 cfs combined with wind can triple the time and work. Late summer flows under 1,200 cfs require more skill to avoid rocks.

18 • Spokane River
(Harvard Road to Plantes Ferry Park)

Distance	• 8 miles
Time	• 2–3 hours
Season	• Virtually year-round
Shuttle	• 9 miles, pavement
Rating	• Class 2
Hazards	• Bridge abutments; powerful eddies and turbulence in high water; rapids
Information	• Spokane County Sheriff marine deputies
Maps	• USGS Spokane NE, Liberty Lake plus Spokane River Centennial Trail map

Flora Rapids on Upper Spokane River (Bart Rayniak photo)

This is the most popular and adventure-filled section of the upper Spokane River. Flora and Sullivan Rapids, both Class 2, are capable of swamping careless or unskilled paddlers. These waters are not as serious as the rapids in Riverside State Park downstream from Spokane, but floaters going from Harvard Road to Plantes Ferry Park can find a section to satisfy a wide variety of paddling skill levels. Kayakers and expert canoeists can be found almost any late spring or early summer evening playing in the waves and holes at Sullivan Rapids.

ACCESS

To reach the put-in from Interstate 90 east of Spokane, take Liberty Lake exit 296. At the intersection, turn north onto Harvard Road. Cross the Spokane River bridge and immediately turn left into the access parking area.

To find the recommended take-out from I-90, take Sullivan exit

291 and head north on Sullivan Road. After crossing over Highway 290 (Trent Avenue), turn left (west) onto Wellesley Road. After driving 2 miles, you will see Plantes Ferry County Park begin where Wellesley bends left and becomes Upriver Drive. The take-out is just west of the main park entrance. To reach this take-out from farther west, take exit 287 off I-90 and drive 2 miles north on Argonne Road. Turn east on Upriver Drive and go 2.2 miles to Plantes Ferry Park.

You can vary this trip by taking advantage of access points at Barker and Sullivan roads, both of which have well-marked exits off I-90 west of Liberty Lake.

PADDLE ROUTE

Flow information • Avista Utilities recording at Post Falls Dam
Historic flows • Average 6,139; maximum 49,800; minimum 67

Spokane County law requires that life vests be worn by anyone floating the Spokane River, even inner tubers. Use common sense in steering clear of hazards posed by bridge abutments. Expect turbulence. Flow rates are very important for this section of river because of changes they make in rapids. Experience is the best teacher, but here are some general guidelines:

- Summer flows below roughly 6,000 cubic feet per second create technical paddling through the rock garden at Flora Rapids. But skilled paddlers can easily negotiate rocks around 2,000 cfs, when the current is less pushy and more conducive to maneuvers.
- Rapids virtually wash out at flows above 15,000 cfs, but large standing waves will be waiting.
- Sullivan Rapids attracts kayaks and play boats in any flow below 20,000 cfs, but most play-boat paddlers simply come upstream from Sullivan Road in very low flows.
- Above roughly 22,000 cfs, water gets into brush along shore. Eddy-outs put paddlers in dangerous proximity of brush and trees. Hydraulics become powerful. Mistakes in strong current of this high, cold water can be disastrous.

Once through Flora Rapids, watch for a big hole on river-right at Sullivan Rapids. Tentative paddlers may want to take the fairly easy tongue leading through left-center of the rapids. Below Sullivan Rapids, keep to center to avoid a hole and rocks on river-left.

Some riffles as well as strong eddies provide the only excitement downstream from Sullivan Road until paddlers reach the old Walk In

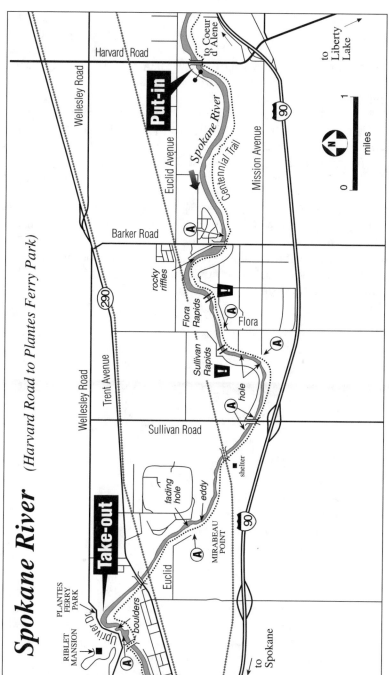

Spokane River *(Harvard Road to Plantes Ferry Park)*

The Wild Zoo site at Mirabeau Point. The area is characterized by fascinating rock formations sloping down to the bend on river-left. Just beyond the large eddy at the bend, kayakers like to play in an unusual hole created only at flows above about 20,000 cfs. The hole grows to a crescendo for several seconds, then fades away, or "greens out," to nothing.

The take-out is at Plantes Ferry Park, where a nice eddy greets paddlers at a dirt launch. Paddlers can enjoy another riffle—turbulent in high flows—and a scenic boulder field below the Riblet Mansion by floating another half mile to a take-out at the Centennial Trail bridge. This is the last riffle before hitting slack water backed up behind Upriver Dam.

Some public land borders the river, most notably along the Centennial Trail on the south shore. Unless they know otherwise, boaters should assume other land above the high water mark is private.

Vandalism and break-ins can be a problem at Spokane River access sites. Leave valuables at home or put them in a waterproof bag and fasten them inside your boat.

19 · Spokane River
(Maple Street to Meenach Bridge)

Distance	• 4 miles
Time	• 1 hour or less
Season	• Virtually year-round
Shuttle	• 4 miles, pavement
Rating	• Class 1-plus
Hazards	• Abandoned bridge pilings
Information	• Spokane County Sheriff marine deputies
Maps	• USGS Spokane NW, plus Spokane County recreation map available from Northwest Map and Travel Book Center in Spokane

A quick fix for that urge to play in a canoe starts on the Spokane River in downtown Spokane just downstream from magnificent Spokane Falls. The trip passes a beach known for occasional nudity and runs through some decent opportunities to catch a brown or rainbow trout. If this sounds too good to be true, it probably is. The nude beach is along a rocky rapids. Boaters should pay attention to the river.

The trip can be paddled in as little as 30 minutes at flows over 6,000 cfs. Houses are common along the river, but some stretches look surprisingly wild for a river in a city. Spokane County laws require paddlers to wear life vests while on the river.

ACCESS

To reach the put-in from Monroe Street in downtown Spokane, drive to just south of the Monroe Street bridge over the Spokane River. Head west (downstream) on Main Street into Peaceful Valley. When you are almost at the bottom of the hill bear right on a one-lane road toward Glover Field. Bear left on Water Street. The put-in is at the grassy park under the Maple Street bridge on the downstream side of the bridge pilings.

Old railroad pilings on Spokane River at Hangman Creek may someday hold a Centennial Trail bridge (Rich Landers photo)

To reach the take-out, continue west on Water Street, past an old casket factory. Turn left at the end of the block onto Ash. Turn right onto Main. Turn left onto Elm. Then turn right onto Clarke.

This is a good point to scout a route through the abandoned bridge pilings in the river. Also, this is the trailhead for paths leading to the beach exposed at the mouth of Hangman Creek in low flows. Runners will recognize the following directions as part of the Bloomsday route that has attracted more than 60,000 runners for the annual fun run on the first Sunday in May.

Drive 0.8 mile and turn right onto Riverside Avenue. Cross Hangman Creek and bear right. At the stop sign, turn right onto Government

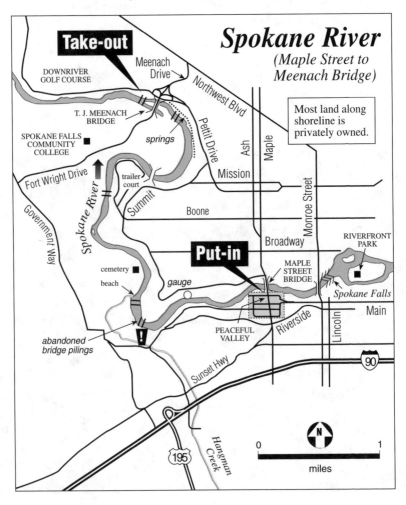

Take-out

DOWNRIVER
GOLF COURSE

Meenach
Drive

Spokane River
(Maple Street to
Meenach Bridge)

Northwest Blvd

T. J. MEENACH
BRIDGE

Most land along
shoreline is
privately owned.

SPOKANE FALLS
COMMUNITY
COLLEGE

springs

Pettit Drive

Ash

Maple

Fort Wright Drive

trailer
court

Mission

Summit

Boone

Monroe Street

Government Way

Spokane River

Broadway

RIVERFRONT
PARK

Put-in

cemetery

beach

gauge

MAPLE
STREET
BRIDGE

Spokane Falls

Main

Lincoln

*abandoned
bridge pilings*

PEACEFUL
VALLEY

Riverside

Sunset Hwy

90

195

Hangman
Creek

N

0   1

miles

Way. Drive nearly 1.5 miles to a stoplight and turn right onto Fort Wright Drive. Go 1.3 miles and bear right immediately after crossing the T. J. Meenach Bridge. (A sign says Riverside State Park.) At the stop sign turn right again, onto Pettit Drive. Head downstream along the Spokane River a quarter mile to a gated access on the river-side of the road.

PADDLE ROUTE

Flow information • Avista Utilities recording at Post Falls Dam
Historic flows • Average 6,139; maximum 49,800; minimum 67

Flow levels play a big role in the appeal of this float. The route is fairly easy in winter flows around 6,000 cfs. Spring flows around 19,000 cfs wash out some rapids but create hard eddylines and serious hydraulics, particularly at the abandoned bridge pilings near the mouth of Hangman Creek. The trickiest paddling could be in late summer when flows drop below 1,200 cfs. The stretch going into the abandoned bridge pilings is rocky, as are the rapids that follow.

Downstream from the mouth of Hangman Creek, the paddling is fairly straightforward. Bigger waves can be skirted if desired. Some public land borders the river, but most of the shoreline is private.

This trip has two take-outs. Look for the first take-out shortly after passing under the Meenach Bridge near a street sewer outlet. Go another 100 yards for the next good take-out, which is somewhat camouflaged in willows. Scout it out during the car shuttle.

Expect to see ducks, mergansers, blue herons, possibly even a bald eagle. The best trout fishing is just above and below the Maple Street bridge and below the three springs that pump cold water into the river just upstream from the Meenach Bridge on river-right.

20 • Little Spokane River

Distance • 6 miles
Time • 3 hours
Season • Virtually year-round
Shuttle • 7 miles, pavement
Rating • Class 1
Hazards • Downed trees, deadheads
Information • Riverside State Park in Spokane
Maps • USGS Nine Mile Falls, Dartford

Floating the Little Spokane River, one can easily forget it's only a short way to the boundary of Eastern Washington's largest city. The riverside habitat attracts a diversity of summering songbird species found in only a few places in the lower 48 states, according to Washington Fish and Wildlife Department research. Mallards and widgeon sputter in back eddies and marshes, while mergansers raft the main channel. Cedar waxwings flock to the river in early spring, painted turtles lounge on logs, beaver trails sneak into the grass, and white-tailed deer snort behind lush riparian plants. Wood ducks nest in boxes maintained by volunteers.

Of all the wildlife, great blue herons have been the most conspicuous. In spring and early summer, the giant birds nest high in cottonwoods at several rookeries along the lower river. The adult birds are bothered by noise and commotion, so canoeists should keep quiet and stay in their boats while passing a rookery.

The yellow iris that line the stream bloom in late May and early June. In the 1920s their seeds spread by wind and current from the estates of wealthy landowners upstream. Though pretty, the iris have displaced native cattails in many places, contributing to the decline of some bird species.

A meandering 6 miles of the stream is open to floaters, from near St. George's School to a developed take-out near the river's confluence with the Spokane River. The trip can be cut in half by launching or taking out at the Painted Rocks access. All three accesses are well marked. Both put-ins require a 100-yard portage to the water.

This stretch of the Little Spokane has no whitewater, and since it is fed in part by the Spokane aquifer, it is passable long after other rivers are too low to float. Possible downed trees, deadheads, two bridges, and several sharp turns present the only navigation challenges. Always check with state park officials during spring runoff, since passage under one residential bridge may be impossible and the gate to the upper put-in could be locked.

ACCESS

To reach the upper put-in from Francis Avenue in Spokane, drive north on Wall Street, veering left at 2 miles onto Waikiki Road. At 3 miles, the pavement ahead becomes Mill Road, and Waikiki turns sharply left. Follow Waikiki 1.3 miles to the turn-off for St. George's School. The put-in is a well-marked parking lot a half mile down this paved road.

To reach the middle access at Painted Rocks, stay on Waikiki instead of turning toward the school. The road crosses the river then

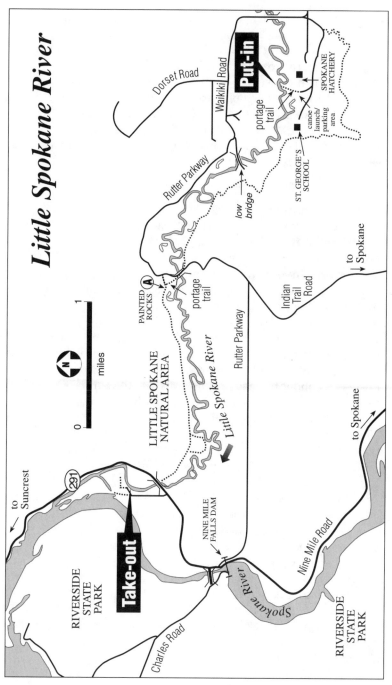

Little Spokane River

bends sharply to the left, becoming Rutter Parkway. It is 3 miles from the St. George's turnoff to the Painted Rocks (named for Indian paintings near the parking lot). A well-beaten path leads from the parking lot paralleling the road to the river put-in.

To reach the take-out from Painted Rocks, go south across the Little Spokane River and uphill to the junction with Indian Trail Road. Turn right, driving another 2 miles on Rutter Parkway. At the stop sign, turn right onto Nine Mile Road (State Highway 291). Go almost 1 mile and turn left (west) at milepost 10 onto the paved access road, which leads a quarter mile to the take-out site.

PADDLE ROUTE

Flow information • USGS Water Resources in Spokane
River gauge • 12431000 near Dartford
Historic flows • Average 293; maximum 3,170; minimum 62

Just downstream from the upper put-in, paddlers see the private campus of St. George's School. Houses also are visible from the river. Most of the shoreline has been purchased by Spokane County and the state of Washington. Rules forbid mucking about by foot along the river shores within the 1,353-acre natural area. This is the only natural area in the State Parks system with special regulations prohibiting swimming, inner tubes, and air mattresses. State rules also prohibit bringing pets, alcoholic beverages, or firearms into the natural area. County rules require everyone on the river to wear life vests.

Paddlers leave the natural area as they pass under the Highway 291 bridge. Swimming is permitted and pets are allowed along the river from here to the confluence with the Spokane River. The take-out is on river-left a short way downstream from the bridge, just before a small set of rapids.

The Little Spokane originates near Newport, Washington. The river and its main fork run through Diamond, Sacheen, Eloika, and Horseshoe Lakes (see trip 21). This last segment is the only significant stretch the public can enjoy. In the 1960s, a foresighted group began lobbying to designate a section of the Little Spokane as a park. During the 1970s and 1980s, Spokane County and the state parks department purchased more than 1,000 acres along the lower river. Some landowners donated their shoreline property to the cause. This lower stretch was added to the state's scenic river system in 1991, giving it added protection.

Fishing is poor in the final miles of the Little Spokane.

More than 40,000 people visit the recreation area annually, and the number keeps growing. The river ecosystem is showing signs of abuse: Not only are herons on the decline, but delicate flowers have been trampled. Except in winter, it is a rare weekend when paddlers are alone on the river. To lessen the impact, members of the Little Spokane Scenic River Task Force suggest leaving the river to the birds and other wildlife during morning hours and in the early spring.

21 • Horseshoe Lake

Distance • 4 miles round trip
Time • Variable
Season • Generally March through October
Shuttle • None
Rating • Flatwater
Hazards • None
Information • Westbrook Resort North of Spokane
Maps • USGS Fan Lake, plus Pend Oreille County map

Horseshoe Lake is one of several lakes and ponds strung like pearls along the Little Spokane River. Sacheen Lake suffers from too many houses, too many boats, and too many people. Weeds threaten to choke Eloika, which is the farthest downstream and suffers the most from sewage, erosion, and the efforts of a farmer who long ago lowered the lake to gain cow pasture.

Steep banks and a lack of potable water have kept most development away from Horseshoe Lake. There are twenty or so houses on the main arm, but none on the eastern half of the horseshoe. At less than 200 acres, Horseshoe could easily be overrun with speedboats. Luckily for paddlers, the speed limit is 5 mph and fishing is notoriously bad.

Visitors are treated to a waterfall that tumbles some 50 feet. The falls, part of the West Branch of the Little Spokane River, is so strong in spring that it hides all boulders in its path. Most summers, it withers to a trickle.

The entire lake can be explored in an hour or two, with less than 4 miles of easy paddling, making this a great family outing.

ACCESS

From U.S. Highway 2 about 20 miles north of Spokane, turn west onto Eloika Lake Road. Drive about 3 miles, then turn north onto

Horseshoe Lake in northeastern Washington (Dan Hansen photo)

Division, a dusty gravel road that changes direction several times. Division becomes Horseshoe Lake Road at slightly more than 2 miles. It is another 5 miles to the lake and a state Fish and Wildlife Department boat launch.

PADDLE ROUTE

To reach the quiet side of the lake, paddle northeast from the launch and through a narrow gap between two points of land (a house sits on each). The waterfall is soon visible on the northern shore. From there, head southeast into the shallow eastern arm, where turtles are common.

With the exception of the launch, all land surrounding Horseshoe Lake is privately owned. So far, the owner has not prevented boaters from visiting the falls. Show your appreciation by picking up the trash left by others. Westbrook Resort, near the boat launch, may offer canoe rentals.

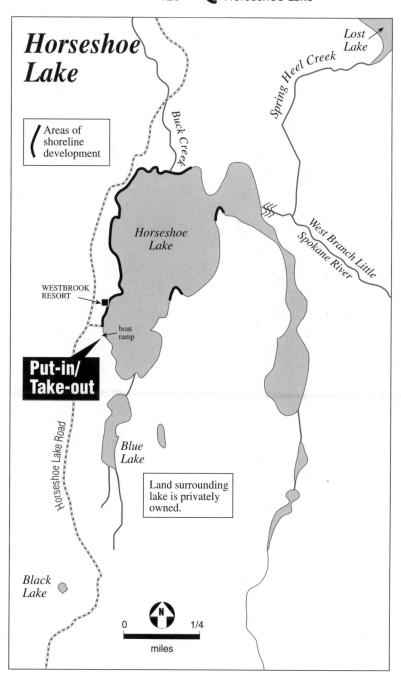

Horseshoe Lake

Areas of shoreline development

Buck Creek

Spring Heel Creek

Lost Lake

West Branch Little Spokane River

Horseshoe Lake

WESTBROOK RESORT

boat ramp

Put-in/ Take-out

Horseshoe Lake Road

Blue Lake

Land surrounding lake is privately owned.

Black Lake

0   N   1/4

miles

22 • Little Pend Oreille Lakes Chain

Distance	•	5 miles round trip
Time	•	2 hours
Season	•	April through October
Shuttle	•	None
Rating	•	Flatwater
Hazards	•	Ski boats
Information	•	Beaver Lodge Resort at Lake Gillette
Maps	•	USGS Lake Gillette, Aladdin Mountain, plus Colville National Forest map

One can only imagine paddling the Little Pend Oreille chain of lakes before roads pierced the Colville National Forest, bringing developers, vacationers, and powerboats to these small gems. Trappers surely found beavers in the four lakes that are linked by the slow-moving Little Pend Oreille River. They certainly found moose, bear, and other wildlife in the forests, meadows, and marshes that surround the lakes.

Today, houses and satellite dishes ring Lakes Sherry, Gillette, Thomas, and Heritage, which range from 26 to 163 acres. Motor size and speed are not restricted, so summer paddlers share the water with flotillas of anglers, water-skiers, and solo jet boats.

Still, the chain is well worth visiting, particularly in fall when most boaters leave and the hills turn amber with Western larch. The channel between Lakes Thomas and Heritage is especially inviting, as it cuts through an expanse of white-flowered lilies. Crowds can be avoided during summer by paddling at first or last light, during moonlit nights, or on cool, cloudy days.

ACCESS

To reach the lakes from Usk, Washington, drive north on State Highway 20. After about 32 miles, the road ahead becomes State Highway 31 and Highway 20 turns to the west, toward Colville. Make the turn and drive 11 miles to Beaver Lodge Resort on Lake Gillette. The lakes also can be reached by following Highway 20 east from Colville.

To reach the only public boat launch, drive 400 feet west from the resort to Little Pend Oreille Lakes Road. Turn left and drive a half mile to the Forest Service campground on Lake Gillette. (There is a second campground on Lake Thomas, less than a mile from the Gillette campground. It has no boat launch, but the portage from the road to a sandy beach is easy.)

PADDLE ROUTE

From Gillette, one can paddle south a short distance to Lake Sherry, or north to Lakes Thomas and Heritage. Round trip from the campground to the far end of Lake Heritage is about 5 miles and can be paddled in less than 2 hours in calm weather.

Lake Gillette of Little Pend Oreille Lakes chain (Dan Hansen photo)

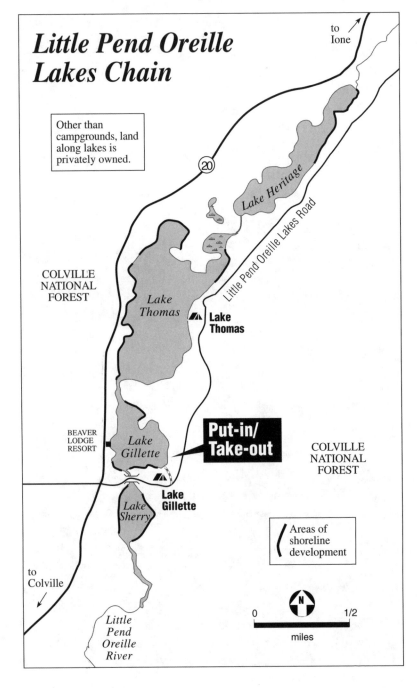

Little Pend Oreille Lakes Chain

Other than campgrounds, land along lakes is privately owned.

to Ione

COLVILLE NATIONAL FOREST

20

Lake Heritage

Little Pend Oreille Lakes Road

Lake Thomas

Lake Thomas

Put-in/ Take-out

COLVILLE NATIONAL FOREST

BEAVER LODGE RESORT

Lake Gillette

Lake Gillette

Lake Sherry

Areas of shoreline development

to Colville

Little Pend Oreille River

0   1/2

miles

N

23 • Pend Oreille River

Distance	•	12 miles
Time	•	5 hours or overnight
Season	•	Generally March through November
Shuttle	•	11.5 miles, mostly pavement
Rating	•	Flatwater, with turbulence at beginning
Hazards	•	Powerful eddies just downstream from Highway 31 bridge; occasional powerboat congestion at Z Canyon
Information	•	Bureau of Land Management in Spokane
Maps	•	USGS Metaline, Metaline Falls, Boundary Dam, plus Colville National Forest map

After negotiating a quarter mile of churning eddies and hydraulics on the Pend Oreille River near Metaline Falls, Washington, paddlers can relax. The flow eases into a scenic canyon spiked with waterfalls, inlets, and shallow caves before backing up into flatwater behind Boundary Dam.

At one stretch, the river constricts into Z Canyon, created by the channel's zigzag through towering rock cliffs. The premier attraction comes near the end of the trip at the wet, windy base of 200-foot Pewee Falls. The falls don't have nearly the volume of Palouse Falls (see trip 12), but they captivate boaters trip after trip.

The Pend Oreille River runs 114 miles from Idaho's Lake Pend Oreille through northeastern Washington and into Canada, where it flows into the Columbia River near Trail, British Columbia. The 12-mile stretch described here is by far the most scenic.

This route was rarely visited by paddling campers as late as the early 1990s. But the secret couldn't last, and several undeveloped campsites had been established by the late 1990s. Developed camping is available at the put-in and take-out. Anglers will find some fishing for trout, bass, and squawfish, although it's not as good as the bass angling upriver in the less scenic stretches near Ione.

ACCESS

The trip starts at Metaline, Washington, which is on State Highway 31 just a few miles downstream from the town of Metaline Falls. At the north end of Metaline, turn east onto Park Street, which winds down three blocks to the city park along the Pend Oreille River. Camping, water, restrooms, and a boat ramp are available.

To reach the take-out, drive north from Metaline on Highway 31 and turn west onto Boundary Road toward Crawford State Park. Drive 10 miles and bear right at the Y for the last mile down to Boundary Dam Campground and the boat launch. (Note that the left fork at

Twin Falls cascade on Pend Oreille River (Rich Landers photo)

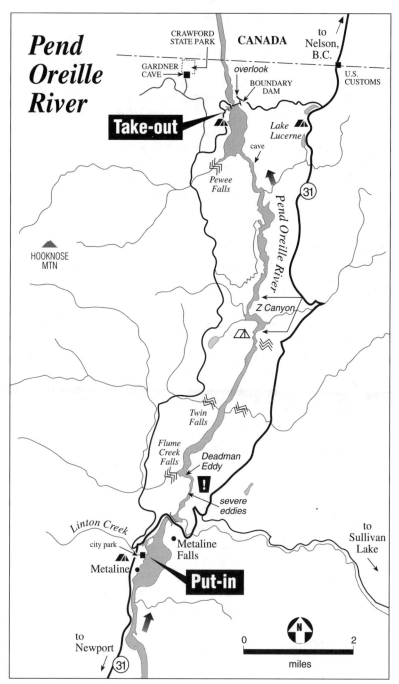

Pend
Oreille
River

the Y goes to Crawford State Park, a worthwhile side trip for guided summer tours into Gardner Cave.)

PADDLE ROUTE

Flow information • Boundary Dam Powerhouse for pool levels
River gauge • 12395500 at Newport
Historic flows • Average 24,930; maximum 135,000; minimum 2,420

When shuttling cars, consider a side trip to the northeast end of the Highway 31 bridge near Metaline Falls for a bird's-eye view of the eddies just downstream. Normally, they look worse than they are. But carelessness near hard eddylines can topple canoes. The origin of the name Deadman Eddy isn't clear, but you don't want to find out the hard way.

As you head downstream, leave time to paddle into several inlets deep enough to hear tumbling waterfalls that are not apparent from the main river. Most of the falls are obvious, however. At one point early in the trip, two cascades unofficially called Twin Falls pour into the Pend Oreille from opposite sides of the canyon.

Mining operations border the river near Metaline and Metaline Falls, but are high on a bench above and out of sight from the river. Some of the land passed early in the trip is privately owned. Lower in the canyon, the land is mostly managed by the U.S. Bureau of Land Management and the Colville National Forest.

A towering gray ridge of rock marks the entrance to Z Canyon. A campsite is on river-left just before the entrance. Listen for boat traffic before making the sharp right turn into the Z.

Boundary Dam is regulated for power production by Seattle City Light. Full pool is 1,990 feet above sea level. It is normal for the summer pool level to fluctuate at least 5 feet a day at the dam or up to one foot a day upstream at Metaline. In winter, fluctuations can be 15 feet a day. Expect fast flows and few places to pull off the river during spring runoff.

Typically, the pool is at its highest level at 6:00 A.M., then gradually goes down as it powers Seattle air conditioners. The lowest pool level of the day usually is around 10:00 P.M. Levels above 1,988 feet obscure entry to nifty shallow caves on river-right before the bay to Pewee Falls. The falls can be approached closely, but not too closely.

Stay river-left when approaching the take-out at the campground. Do not go beyond the boat launch. Buoys mark the danger area near the gates of Boundary Dam.

24 • Columbia River
(Canada to Northport)

Distance	•	10 miles
Time	•	3 hours
Season	•	Virtually year-round
Shuttle	•	12 miles, mostly pavement
Rating	•	Class 2
Hazards	•	Unpredictable currents, scattered whitewater, strong eddylines
Information	•	Lake Roosevelt National Recreation Area in Kettle Falls
Maps	•	USGS Northport, Boundary, plus Lake Roosevelt National Recreation Area map

Tourists from every industrialized nation have visited Grand Coulee Dam, and growing crowds of boaters ply Lake Roosevelt, the reservoir behind the dam. But just upstream from the slack water is a short stretch of the Columbia River that often is overlooked, and still runs free. While there are no life-threatening rapids like those lost behind dams, this trip gives paddlers a sense for the power and majesty of the Columbia that challenged early explorers.

Boaters should be aware that while the Columbia looks tame from shore, it is possessed of unpredictable currents. The river is so broad that most of the rapids can be avoided. Still, there are powerful whirl-pools, eddies, and crosscurrents that can jolt a canoe or toss water over the gunwales. Capsizing can mean a long, exhausting swim in frigid water. More boaters die on the Columbia than on any other water in Washington, including Puget Sound. Beginning paddlers should not venture onto the river without several boats and more experienced companions.

ACCESS

Paddlers should leave a shuttle vehicle at the boat launch in Northport, where the trip ends. The town is on the east side of the river on State Highway 25. To reach the boat launch, veer right just before the highway crosses over the Columbia. Follow a well-marked road past a sawmill to the city park at the base of the bridge. Camping in vehicles is allowed at the park, but tents are not allowed.

To reach the put-in from Northport, drive north 11 miles on the

Northport–Boundary Road (State Highway 251) to the tiny village of Boundary. Turn left on Waneta Road, which winds downhill about a mile to the Waneta border crossing. About 100 feet shy of the U.S. Border Patrol building, at the point where the guard rail ends, a dirt road leads about 100 yards to an old building site at the Great Northern Railroad tracks. Paddlers can park in the clearing, which is federal land, and carry their gear over the tracks and down an embankment to a prominent eddy where the trip begins. The route is easy to find despite the lack of a trail. Near the put-in is an informal campsite and fire ring.

PADDLE ROUTE

Flow information • USGS Water Resources in Spokane
River gauge • 12436500 at Grand Coulee Dam
Historic flows • Average 108,000; maximum 638,000; minimum 14,900

From the put-in, paddlers look out at an island that parts the river, creating some of the diciest whitewater of the trip. Unfortunately for thrillseekers, it would take a tremendous effort to cross 100 yards of strong current to reach the froth. The hillside beyond the island, on the river's western shore, draws deer, bears, and other wildlife early and late in the day.

Farther downstream, the west bank is dotted with occasional houses and trailers, but the east bank remains relatively undeveloped. Paddlers are treated to views of lushly forested mountains and a riparian zone rich with deciduous trees and shrubs. The railroad tracks cross numerous ravines and gorges on picturesque wooden trestles. The highway shows itself only occasionally, and the sound of cars is drowned by the rush of the water.

Fishing can be good at times for rainbow trout. This free-flowing stretch of river even holds a few remaining native cutthroat trout, which, if caught, should be gently released.

Boaters who want a longer trip than the one described here may continue to the China Bend boat launch, 10 miles downstream from Northport. Most of the additional miles are slack water when Lake Roosevelt is at summer levels, but often are free-flowing when the reservoir is drawn down in spring to make room for snowmelt. Beware of strong, unpredictable currents and sometimes dangerous whirlpools in the Little Dalles, where the river rushes through a narrow gorge. There is little opportunity for escape if a boat capsizes in this isolated stretch of river.

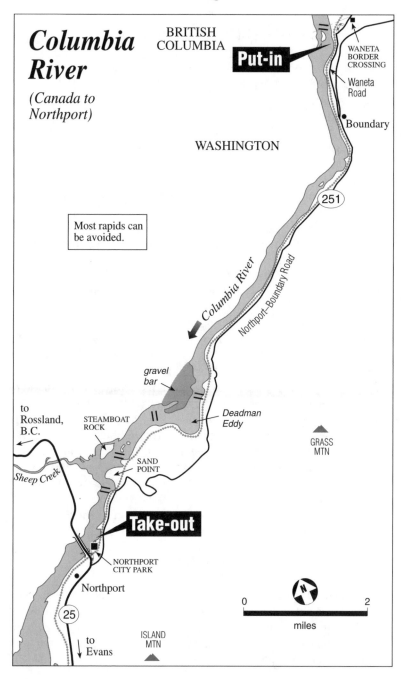

Columbia River

(Canada to Northport)

BRITISH COLUMBIA

Put-in

WANETA BORDER CROSSING

Waneta Road

• Boundary

WASHINGTON

251

Most rapids can be avoided.

Columbia River

Northport–Boundary Road

gravel bar

to Rossland, B.C.

STEAMBOAT ROCK

Deadman Eddy

GRASS MTN

Sheep Creek

SAND POINT

Take-out

NORTHPORT CITY PARK

Northport

25

to Evans

ISLAND MTN

0   2

miles

N

25 • Kettle River
(Washington)

Distance	•	12 miles
Time	•	3 hours
Season	•	Generally March through April, mid-June through early August
Shuttle	•	9 miles, pavement and gravel
Rating	•	Class 1
Hazards	•	Possessive landowners
Information	•	Lake Roosevelt National Recreation Area in Kettle Falls
Maps	•	USGS Laurier and Orient

Summer brings all manner of craft to the Kettle River in northeastern Washington. Inner tubes bob in the current along with rafts that serve as little more than floating platforms for parties. For canoeists, this trip is a fine alternative to staying home when most rivers are too low to paddle.

All is not well on the Kettle, however. In response to moves to protect the river under the national Wild and Scenic River Act, the Washington State Legislature handed over control of the Kettle to Ferry and Stevens Counties in 1990. The counties consider the riverbed private property, which means anyone caught standing on an island or the shoreline is considered a trespasser, even if he or she is below the ordinary high-water mark. Only one other stream in Eastern Washington—the Little Spokane River above the publicly owned natural area—has such restrictive access (see trip 20). Public land on the Kettle is scarce. Canoeists should be careful where they stop for shore breaks.

This trip starts just shy of the Canadian border and ends in the town of Orient, Washington. The river flows through open pastures and shaded forests. Visitors have a good chance of seeing white-tailed deer—in fact, deer are an after-dark hazard on area highways.

ACCESS

From the town of Kettle Falls, Washington, follow U.S. Highway 395 west over the Columbia River, then drive north about 20 miles on Highway 395. At milepost 260, turn right into Orient and follow the town's main street about a half mile to a bridge over the Kettle River. The steep take-out—it may require two or more people to haul a canoe up the bank—is just upstream from the bridge, on the east side of the river.

To reach the put-in from Orient, continue north on Highway 395. Turn right onto Deep Creek Road, which is just past milepost 269 and less than a mile from the Canadian border. The gravel road twists downhill about a mile before coming to the bank of the Kettle. Follow it another mile to a bridge over the river.

Waiting for lower water on Kettle River near Orient, Washington (Dan Hansen photo)

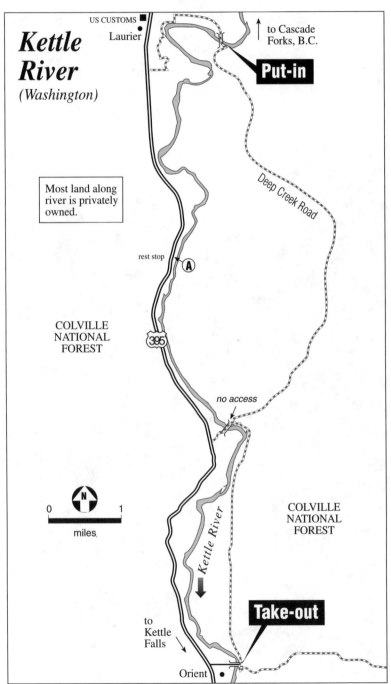

Kettle River
(Washington)

US CUSTOMS ■
• Laurier

↑ to Cascade
Forks, B.C.

Put-in

Most land along
river is privately
owned.

Deep Creek Road

rest stop ─ Ⓐ

COLVILLE
NATIONAL
FOREST

395

no access

0 ───── 1
miles

N

Kettle River

COLVILLE
NATIONAL
FOREST

Take-out

to
Kettle
Falls

Orient •

For years, river runners have used a rough path on the south side of the bridge to launch their inner tubes and boats. No one bothered to check whether the land was public or private. In 1997, Ferry and Stevens Counties were installing a new bridge, and the exact width of the public easement was not yet settled; it may be no wider than the bridge itself. Most likely, paddlers are safe if they don't stray from the rip-rap on either side of the bridge; just be aware that the rules may change.

Between Orient and Deep Creek Road, just past milepost 266, a highway turn-out provides an alternate access for those who would like to shorten the trip. It also is a safe spot for a shore break during the paddle. Road maps show the turnout as a rest stop, but there are no restrooms or picnic tables, just a garbage barrel.

PADDLE ROUTE

Flow information • USGS Water Resources in Spokane
River gauge • 12404500 at Laurier
Historic flows • Average 2,878; maximum 35,000; minimum 70

For best boating, look for flows no greater than 4,000 cubic feet per second. Traditionally, the best flows are in March, April, and July. Spring runoff usually chases sane boaters off the river during May and most of June, when flows sometimes top 20,000 cfs. (The average is 12,000 cfs in May and 9,000 cfs in June.) Fall and winter can provide fine paddling, although the river often is low. The lowest water of the year normally comes in January, when the river's sources in Canada are frozen.

Camping is available at the National Park Service's Kettle River and Kamloops Islands campgrounds near the confluence of the Kettle and Columbia Rivers.

The Washington Fish and Wildlife Department is trying to restore quality trout fishing to the Kettle River with special regulations. Check the current state fishing pamphlet.

BRITISH COLUMBIA

26 • Kettle River
(British Columbia)

Distance	•	30 miles
Time	•	10 hours
Season	•	Generally mid-June and July
Shuttle	•	24 miles, pavement and gravel
Rating	•	Class 1
Hazards	•	Strainers, debris
Information	•	Kettle River Provincial Park near Rock Creek (summer only); Ministry of Parks, West Kootenay District in Nelson
Maps	•	Canada EMR Almond Mountain 82 E/2, Greenwood 82 E/7

An international stream, the 220-mile long Kettle River has its genesis in the West Kootenay region of British Columbia. It dips into Washington, turns north again into Canada, then makes one more border crossing for its final 33-mile run to the Columbia River near the town of Kettle Falls, Washington (see trip 25). In the process, it offers many miles of paddling opportunities.

The trip described here starts in a forest of mixed conifers, then flows into a broad, lush valley of dairy farms, cattle ranches, and alfalfa fields. Deer are amazingly abundant on the farms, and beavers are busy felling the cottonwoods that grow thick along the river. There are no notable rapids during normal river flows. The lower 4 miles are popular with locals on inner tubes.

Low water on the Kettle River (Dan Hansen photo)

ACCESS

Kettle River Provincial Park makes a good base for a weekend of exploring, or a good take-out after a day of paddling. To reach the park from Curlew, Washington, drive northwest along the Kettle River for 16 miles on Route 501, to the Ferry/Midway border crossing (open 8:00 A.M. to 5:00 P.M.). One mile north of the international border, in the town of Midway, turn left on Provincial Highway 3. Twelve miles from Midway, turn right onto Route 33 in the town of Rock Creek. It is 4 miles from Rock Creek to the provincial park, which has ample camping and good river access through the picnic area.

Depending on the length of trip one desires, many options for launching are found upstream of the park.

To reach the closest put-in, drive 4 miles north from the park on Route 33 to Westbridge. Just before the highway crosses the West Fork of the Kettle River, turn left onto Westbridge Road, which leads a few hundred feet to the river and the put-in at the base of the bridge. This launch is about a quarter mile upstream from the confluence of the West Fork and the main Kettle River.

Other access points are on the main Kettle, along Christian Valley Road, which starts in Westbridge and has kilometer markers showing the distance from that small village:

- The first Christian Valley access is just shy of the 8 km marker at Fiva Creek Road. Two or three cars can be parked on the east side of the river, where a steep trail leads to the water.
- At 18 km, the road comes to the river's edge, providing decent access with parking for several cars on the road shoulder.
- At 27 km, the road is again next to the river. A spur to the east immediately crosses the river and provides an obvious parking area and good place to launch.
- Canyon Creek campground, at 32 km, is the final access on the gentle portion of the river. Upstream is a gorge with rapids too dicey for paddlers who lack whitewater skills and equipment. The campground is relatively undeveloped, with just two rough campsites and a pit toilet.

PADDLE ROUTE

Flow information • Water Survey Canada in Penticon

River gauge • 08NN026 above Westbridge, 08NN003 on the West Fork

Historic flows • Average not available; maximum 15,925; minimum not available (35 on West Fork)

One good paddling option is the 4-hour trip from Canyon Creek to Fiva Creek, which offers a variety of scenery and excellent wildlife viewing. A group interested in a leisurely weekend could complete that trip one morning, then make a second trip from Fiva Creek to Kettle River Provincial Park the next. The itinerary would provide plenty

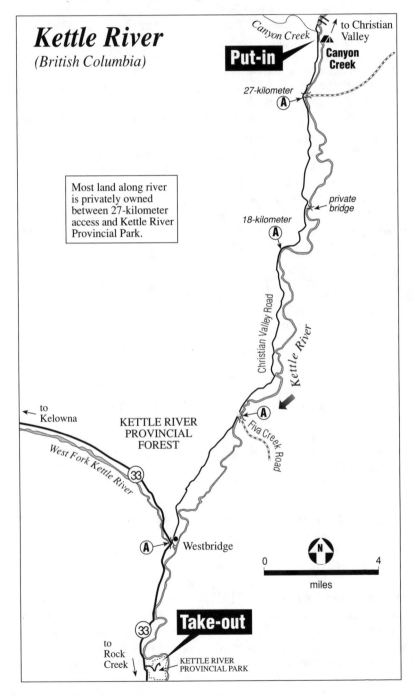

Kettle River
(British Columbia)

Put-in

Canyon Creek

to Christian Valley

Canyon Creek

27-kilometer Ⓐ

Most land along river is privately owned between 27-kilometer access and Kettle River Provincial Park.

private bridge

18-kilometer Ⓐ

Christian Valley Road

Kettle River

to Kelowna

KETTLE RIVER PROVINCIAL FOREST

Ⓐ

Fiva Creek Road

West Fork Kettle River

33

Ⓐ Westbridge

N

0   4

miles

33

Take-out

to Rock Creek

KETTLE RIVER PROVINCIAL PARK

of paddling and sight-seeing for adults, plus ample shore time for younger members of the party.

The provincial government maintains a river gauge on the main Kettle River above its confluence with the smaller West Fork. Another gauge is on the West Fork itself. Readings from the two gauges must be combined, then converted to cfs, to accurately determine the flow below the confluence. The gauge on the main Kettle does not operate in winter.

In spring, the river is high and brown, reaching a peak of nearly 6,000 cubic feet per second during a typical May. July flows average a tame 1,500 cfs. By August, the river usually drops to about 400 cfs. Most winters reduce the flow to a trickle.

27 • Granby River

Distance •	12 miles
Time •	3–4 hours
Season •	Generally March through July
Shuttle •	10 miles, pavement
Rating •	Class 1 with avoidable Class 2
Hazards •	Strainers, possible logjams; drop and turbulence near old dam site; rattlesnakes
Information •	Wild Waves Sport Shop in Christina Lake
Maps •	Canada EMR Grand Forks 82 E/1

Only skeletons remain from the railroads, smelter, and dam that once rumbled, belched, and clogged the Granby River Valley near Grand Forks, British Columbia. May they rest in peace. At its source, the river remains undefiled. The Granby begins in a roadless wilderness of the southern Monashee Mountains and flows freely for 65 miles to its confluence with the Kettle River. The paddling options here attract a spectrum ranging from whitewater kayaking junkies to little kids in inflatable duckies.

The Granby's upper reaches have no road or trail access. The middle section is the realm of expert kayakers who can handle unpredictable waters such as the "Staircase" and "S-Curves," where serious drops are complicated by narrow rock gorges and logjams.

The lower Granby, however, is both easily accessible and accommodating to less experienced paddlers. But the floating season is short. Lingering winter weather can foil early-season excursions in this

Surfing Spit Wally's Hole on Granby River (Rich Landers photo)

mountainous area. Peak runoff can raise the river to unsafe conditions sometime in late May or early June. By the end of July, the combination of low flows and irrigation pumps leaves the river too low for canoeing, although inflatables can continue to slide over the rocks.

Prime time is late June and the first few weeks of July, when the water warms; flows are just high enough for good paddling but low enough to expose the numerous sandy beaches.

Three bridges across the lower Granby are roughly at 10, 17, and 28 road miles upstream from Grand Forks, offering access points and options for paddling different stretches of Class 1 water. The scenery improves and the river becomes progressively more solitary as you head up the drainage. But the higher you go, the more susceptible the river is to logjams and strainers.

ACCESS

This trip begins at Ten-mile Bridge, also known locally as Hummingbird Bridge. The put-in is accessible by paved roads on both sides of the river.

East side: Drive into Grand Forks on Provincial Highway 3. At the east side of the bridge over the Granby River, turn north (upstream) onto Granby Road. Drive 1.4 miles and note a narrow, unmarked gravel road dropping down to the river just north of the black slag piles. This leads to the old dam site, an undeveloped picnic area, and a sometimes clothes-optional river access locally known as Slag Beach. Continuing north on Granby Road, pass another river access at 5.3 miles. At nearly 10 miles from Grand Forks, bear left at a Y to the bridge. The put-in is on the upstream side, river-right.

West side: From Highway 3 at the west edge of Grand Forks, turn north onto North Fork Road. Drive 7.5 miles and note the right turn onto Niagara Town Site Road, which leads down to a river access. Continue another 2 miles up the North Fork Road to the bridge put-in.

To reach the take-out, turn north off Highway 3 in Grand Forks and head north on Second Street (just west of the Granby River bridge). Turn right (east) at the stop, then bend left (north) onto Riverside Drive. At 83rd Street, turn right and into Barbara Ann Park, where there is parking, lawn, and a sandy beach along the river.

PADDLE ROUTE

Flow information • Water Survey Canada in Penticton
River gauge • 08NN002 at Grand Forks
Historic flows • Average 1,071; maximum 13,475; minimum 8

A 20-mile loop drive from Grand Forks to Ten-mile Bridge via the North Fork and Granby Roads offers a neat way to get acquainted with this trip and scout the river. Bighorn sheep can sometimes be seen on the rocky slopes above. White-tailed deer are more common than people in the Granby Valley early on a summer morning or late in the evening as they feed in the vast bottomland meadows. The deer take refuge in the aspens, cottonwoods, and pines during midday, while playful otters are a possible sight anytime.

The river meanders through this broad section of the valley, sometimes braiding into channels. Small channels can be plugged with logjams, posing danger in high flows for paddlers who aren't paying attention downstream. In low flows, the smaller channels might simply run short of water.

The most challenging sections on this stretch include a big eddy followed by a stretch of riffles and rapids at Niagara. The last challenge begins at the old dam site. Look for an island of rock rubble and pilings in the middle of the river. The left channel has a serious drop. The right channel usually produces an easy tongue of flow leading down to a bend and several hundred yards of continuous riffles. At certain flow levels, it is possible to take on water near Slag Beach.

At the first sight of the big black slag piles, carefully scan the river-left half of the stream. Spit Wally's Hole doesn't look like much from upstream, but paddlers who aren't ready for serious surfing should give it a wide berth. At certain levels, this is a "keeper" hole that has been known to dump more than a few boaters and hold them in its frothy grasp. The hole is easily avoidable by staying river-right.

The take-out is at the calm water and beach at Barbara Ann Park. A set of gauges at the upstream end of the park can be useful to boaters who regularly paddle the Granby, although they are difficult to read. The lower river paddles well at roughly 1 to 2.5 meters on these gauges, but these are not official measurements. A gauge records river flows, but real-time flow information has been difficult to obtain from government sources.

Undeveloped campsites can be found along and near the Granby River, but the only official campgrounds are in the upper reaches, beyond the paved road above Burrell Creek. The first of several camping areas is nearly 30 miles upstream from Grand Forks. The rough road that goes upstream to Traverse Creek led to the only significant trail into the upper reaches of the Granby areas when it was protected as a 100,000-acre wilderness in 1995.

Rainbow trout inhabit the Granby, but large fish don't survive well in the lower stretches because of the skimpy flows that plague the river for much of the year. Upstream, where access is difficult, streamside habitat is healthy, and summer flows are cooler, the trout fishing can be superb for anglers with the mettle to get there.

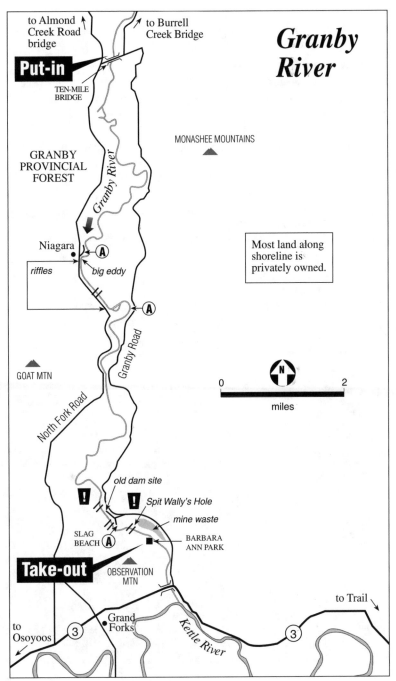

Granby River

to Almond
Creek Road
bridge

to Burrell
Creek Bridge

Put-in

TEN-MILE
BRIDGE

MONASHEE MOUNTAINS

GRANBY
PROVINCIAL
FOREST

Granby River

Niagara

(A)

riffles

big eddy

(A)

Granby Road

GOAT MTN

Most land along
shoreline is
privately owned.

North Fork Road

N

0 — 2
miles

old dam site

Spit Wally's Hole

mine waste

SLAG
BEACH (A)

BARBARA
ANN PARK

Take-out

OBSERVATION
MTN

to Trail

to
Osoyoos

3

Grand
Forks

Kettle River

3

28 • Slocan River

Distance	•	24 miles
Time	•	5–8 hours
Season	•	Generally April through mid-November
Shuttle	•	20 miles, pavement
Rating	•	Class 1, with some Class 2
Hazards	•	Pilings from old logging operations scattered along river; logjams; afternoon wind
Information	•	Lemon Creek Lodge south of Slocan
Maps	•	Canada EMR Passmore 82F/5

The Slocan River flows out of Slocan Lake (see trip 29) in the rugged Kootenay Range and runs 37 miles to its confluence with the Kootenay River upstream from Castlegar. The valley bustled during the gold mining boom in the 1890s. The modern attraction is the scenery and outdoor activities in clear waters that originate in Valhalla and Kokanee Glacier Provincial Parks.

The Slocan offers numerous options to accommodate long or short trips. The lower 3 miles downstream from Crescent Valley hold Class

Eddied-out on Slocan River (Rich Landers photo)

3-plus rapids that delight whitewater boaters. The upper river from Slocan Lake to Lemon Creek passes through a wildlife-rich slough, but tends to be plagued with logjams. The trip described below features the middle portion of the river, which offers the safest adventure for average paddlers.

ACCESS

From Castlegar, British Columbia, drive north on Provincial Highway 3A toward Nelson 11.8 miles and turn west (left) onto Provincial Highway 6 toward Slocan. Take a vehicle odometer reading at this junction. The take-out for this trip is 0.8 mile west on Highway 6 at the south edge of Crescent Valley. Parking is available on the river side of the highway. A steep trail leads down to a beach.

To reach the put-in, continue upstream on Highway 6. River access points along the way include (mileages are from the junction of Highways 6 and 3A): the bridge just north of Crescent Valley off Pass Creek Road, 1.5 miles; the Slocan Park bridge, 7.5 miles; the Passmore bridge off Upper Passmore Road, 9.3 miles; the Vallican bridge, 11 miles; Winlaw Bridge off Winlaw Bridge Road, 16.5 miles.

The put-in for this trip is at Perry's Bridge, off Perry's Back Road, 21.2 miles north of the junction, or 2.5 miles south of Lemon Creek.

PADDLE ROUTE

Flow information	• West Kootenay Power, or Water Survey Canada in Nelson
River gauge	• 08NJ013 near Crescent Valley
Historic flows	• Average 3,087; maximum 24,290; minimum 297

The Slocan River is broad and gentle with splendid views upstream and down from the put-in to Winlaw Nature Park on river-right. The park has a lawn, a covered pavilion, restrooms, and boardwalks. This is an excellent stop for a picnic and swim. Despite the glaciers in the mountains above, the Slocan is remarkably warm by early July. Winlaw Nature Park could be used as an access, but paddlers would have to portage 200 yards to the river. Whitewater stretches can be avoided by pulling out at Winlaw Bridge, just downstream from the park.

After paddling under Winlaw Bridge, begin a long, fun stretch of rapids perhaps ranging up to Class 2 in very high or very low water conditions. Other than possible logjams, deadheads, and strainers, the floating is fairly routine from here to a nifty sand beach downstream from the confluence of Little Slocan River near Passmore. At a bend

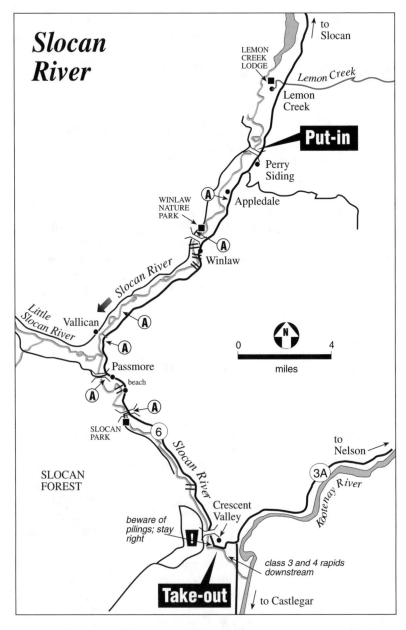

Slocan River

below the sand beach, large rocks create eddies and holes; good paddlers view the water here as a playground, but it could cause trouble for novice paddlers. Stay river-right to avoid the obstacles.

The stretch from Passmore to the Slocan Park bridge has several rapids ranging between Class 1 and Class 2.

The only notable concern downstream from Slocan Park is a series of pilings that block the left channel at the last big bend before the take-out at Crescent Valley. Stay river-right around the pilings. After rounding the bend and passing the last of the pilings, steer toward river-left to prepare for the take-out. A series of rocks at the take-out could cause problems for novices in swifter early summer flows. Scout this take-out during the vehicle shuttle.

The river is bordered mostly by private land with no legitimate camping opportunities. Paddlers can find plenty of shoreline beaches during summer for stopping. The sand beach at the take-out is a popular local swimming hole.

Slocan River flows generally peak in June. The best paddling on this stretch is before or after peak runoff. The river can get quite low in late August. The easiest floating is at flows around 4,500 cubic feet per second—enough to cover most rocks without creating severe hydraulics. Higher flows present more concern for possible logjams and strainers. Lower flows expose more rocks, requiring more maneuvering at a number of points.

The Slocan Valley has numerous attractions, including Nakusp Hot Springs Resort north of Slocan Lake, an abandoned 1890s gold mining town called Sandon, and a museum in New Denver for recalling the local World War II Japanese internment camp.

29 · Slocan Lake

Distance •	23 miles
Time •	2–3 days
Season •	Generally March through November
Shuttle •	30 miles, pavement; optional 5 miles gravel
Rating •	Flatwater
Hazards •	Unpredictable winds; bears
Information •	Valhalla Provincial Park headquarters in Nelson
Maps •	Canada EMR 82F/13, 82F/14 and 82K/3, plus Valhalla Provincial Park brochure

Sand beaches and isolated campsites dot the rugged, roadless, and mostly wilderness western shoreline of British Columbia's Slocan Lake. The water is clear enough to see paddle shadows 20 feet deep. Trails

Wilderness beach on west shore of Slocan Lake (Rich Landers photo)

lead from the lake to waterfalls, alpine lakes, and spongy lichen-carpeted old-growth forests. A highway and three small towns are carved out along the east shore, but the lake is just big enough for paddlers to feel remarkably alone if they hug the western shoreline and the boundary of Valhalla Provincial Park.

The name Valhalla comes from the magnificent mythological palace for the bravest of slain Norse warriors. The views are inspiring from the lake. The best of the Valhalla, however, is waiting for those who hike the high-country trails to views of 9,000-foot points such as Mount Dag and Gimli, Asgard, and Gladsheim Peaks.

ACCESS

From Castlegar, British Columbia, drive 12 miles north on Provincial Highway 3A. At the junction, turn onto Provincial Highway 6 toward Slocan and continue north about 28 miles. Turn left into Slocan.

Go right at the first paved road, then left onto Fletcher Street, following signs to the village park and boat launch at the end of Main Street. The park's boat launch is the put-in for this trip.

To reach take-outs at the north end of the lake, continue north on Highway 6. Drive through New Denver and go 10 miles. Turn left toward the bedroom community of Hills on Bonanza Road, which forks at a bridge across Shannon Creek. Choose from two options:

- Follow a paved road left a short distance to Alvorez Road, which leads to a day-use beach. Traditionally, overnight parking has been tolerated here but camping is not allowed. Asking permission is recommended.
- Turn right at the fork, leaving the pavement, and head up Shannon Creek Road. Go left at another fork, following signs to Wragge Beach Forest Campground (5 miles from the Shannon Creek bridge).

PADDLE ROUTE

Where to start an end-to-end paddle tour on Slocan Lake is debatable. The prevailing wind reportedly comes from the north, but experienced paddlers say winds from the south are common.

Big-time tourism has been slow to find Slocan Lake. Services in the area tend to be mom-and-pop operations that generally include canoe rentals and accommodations.

Boat launches and campgrounds are found at Slocan, Silverton, New Denver, and Rosebery. In addition to Wragge Beach Campground, at least nine other primitive campsites can be found along the west shore where there is no road access. Some have sand beaches, others are rocky. Nemo Creek Falls trailhead is popular with power-boaters, making the beach one of the busiest areas on the west shore. Evans Creek Camp, accessible by trail from Slocan, has a three-sided log shelter. Cove Creek Beach has a public cabin with room for up to six people.

Between campsites, the shoreline is rugged with granite outcroppings. Pictographs are found on rock walls on the west side of the lake in at least three places. The shoreline is lined with a mixed forest including cedar, hemlock, larch, grand fir, pine, lodgepole, spruce, yew, alder, birch, poplar, willow, and mountain ash. On the shore near Cove Creek, you can even find some ponderosa pines thriving at the northern extreme of the species' range.

The Valhallas are well-known grizzly country. Designated campsites have poles, usually near an outhouse, for hanging food. Watch

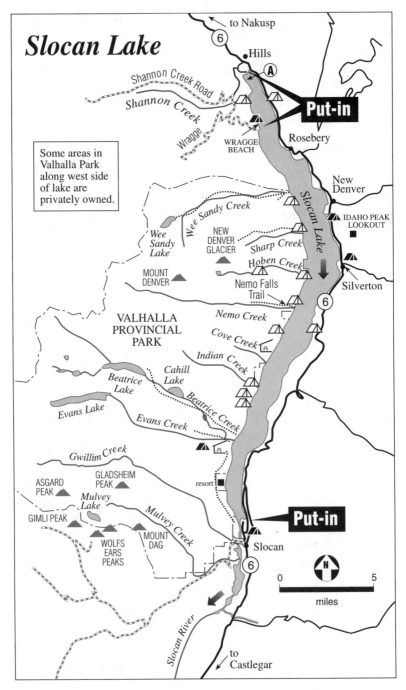

Slocan Lake

to Nakusp

6

Hills

(A)

Shannon Creek Road

Shannon Creek

Wragge

Put-in

WRAGGE BEACH

Rosebery

New Denver

Some areas in Valhalla Park along west side of lake are privately owned.

Wee Sandy Creek

Slocan Lake

IDAHO PEAK LOOKOUT

Wee Sandy Lake

NEW DENVER GLACIER

Sharp Creek

Hoben Creek

MOUNT DENVER

Nemo Falls Trail

Silverton

6

VALHALLA PROVINCIAL PARK

Nemo Creek

Cove Creek

Indian Creek

Cahill Lake

Beatrice Lake

Beatrice Creek

Evans Lake

Evans Creek

Gwillim Creek

ASGARD PEAK

GLADSHEIM PEAK

Mulvey Lake

GIMLI PEAK

Mulvey Creek

WOLFS EARS PEAKS

MOUNT DAG

resort

Put-in

Slocan

6

0   5
miles

N

Slocan River

to Castlegar

for loons and ospreys. Anglers can catch rainbow trout, kokanee, and whitefish.

Although temperatures can be cold in winter, Slocan Lake rarely freezes, which made it a water highway for early-day mine and timber company barges. Rain is common every month of the year. Snow typically sticks to the shoreline in November and melts by April.

The spectacular collection of peaks and alpine lakes in the mountains ranging up from the lake were protected in the 122,500-acre Valhalla Provincial Park in 1983. At nearly 3 miles long, Evans Lake is huge by high-mountain lake standards.

The park has not been as heavily used as Canada's more famous national parks to the north, primarily because the roads leading to the Slocan Valley are narrow and windy, and few access roads and trails have been developed in the park itself. Visitation, however, has been steadily growing. Access fees and park permits for campers are a future possibility. Check with park officials. Dogs are allowed in the park, but must be leashed. Fires are permitted only in designated campsites. Rangers recommend using only driftwood.

30 · Elk River

Distance	•	17 miles
Time	•	6 hours
Season	•	Generally July through October
Shuttle	•	15 miles, pavement
Rating	•	Class 1-plus
Hazards	•	Possible logjams; high water during runoff
Information	•	Fernie Chamber of Commerce
Maps	•	Canada EMR Fernie 82/G

The Elk River gushes with water for much of the year, but only a trickle of boats finds way to the British Columbia stream. Most of the use is by rafts or drift boats oared by anglers keying in to the river's native cutthroat trout. The fishing can be good in late summer and fall—so good that anglers don't invest the time a paddler might devote to appreciating the scenery. From the cottonwood-lined shores up to spectacular peaks, the Elk is an eyeful.

The river above Hosmer is smaller, with tighter turns and a steeper gradient. The large but graceful hoofed creatures for which the river is named make their home at the river's headwaters. The river below

Mount Hosmer looms above Elk River near Fernie
(Rich Landers photo)

Morrissey offers generally good floating, with some slack water to reach the take-out at the bridge near the dam at Elko.

This trip features the most scenic portion of the 119-mile river, with stunning views of Mount Hosmer and other peaks. It flows through Fernie, a small ski-resort town where paddlers can easily eddy out for food or supplies. The river is especially scenic in late September and early October, when cottonwoods and aspens turn brilliant yellow. Since the river flows don't tend to settle down until the end of July, the fishing is best from August through mid-October.

ACCESS

The undeveloped put-in is just downstream from Hosmer. Check the odometer at the bridge over the Elk River at the *north* end of Fernie. Drive 6.2 miles north on Provincial Highway 3. Cross the bridge over the river just south of Hosmer. At the first safe opportunity, make a U-turn and drive back south on Highway 3. This is necessary for a better entry to the crude access road that parallels the highway barricade. The access is on the downstream side of the highway bridge.

To reach the undeveloped take-out, check the odometer at the Elk River bridge on the *south* end of Fernie. Take Highway 3 south 8.5 miles and turn east on Morrissey Road. (The turnoff is 9.5 miles north of Elko.) Just before the Morrissey bridge, bear right onto a dirt road to a rough boat launch and parking area.

PADDLE ROUTE

Flow information • Water Survey Canada in Cranbrook
River gauge • 08NK002 at Fernie
Historic flows • Average 1,627; maximum 21,700;
minimum 210

Massive 1995 floods rearranged the river channel shown on any previous map. The post-flood river wound up being straighter than it was before 1995. But because of the cottonwoods along this river, there is always a chance for logjams that could create new bends and channels year by year.

This trip begins across the highway from the flank of Mount Hosmer, a mass of rock and snow that peeks in and out of view for the first half of the trip. One of the best views is looking upstream between the two bridges in Fernie, where one also looks up at stunning Three Sisters Peaks.

From Hosmer to Fernie, paddlers must negotiate a couple of snaky turns, plus one potentially upsetting drop as the stream approaches the railroad grade about two-thirds of the way to Fernie. The drop generally is not a factor in flows over 1,000 cubic feet per second. But rocks can protrude almost unavoidably at flows under 800 cfs. Generally, flows around 800 to 1,000 cfs are ideal for paddling the entire trip. Higher flows can intensify Class 1-plus spots between Fernie and Morrissey. Lower flows expose rocks in riffles.

The float from Hosmer to Fernie takes about 2.5 hours. It is possible

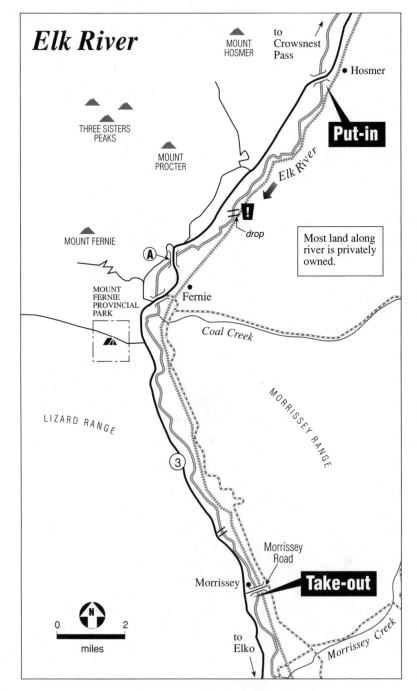

Elk River

MOUNT HOSMER

to Crowsnest Pass

● Hosmer

Put-in

THREE SISTERS PEAKS

MOUNT PROCTER

Elk River

! drop

Most land along river is privately owned.

MOUNT FERNIE

Ⓐ

MOUNT FERNIE PROVINCIAL PARK

● Fernie

Coal Creek

LIZARD RANGE

MORRISSEY RANGE

③

Morrissey Road

Take-out

Morrissey ●

N

0 — 2
miles

to Elko

Morrissey Creek

to pull out at either bridge in Fernie. The northwest side of the upstream bridge is better suited to parking vehicles. This trip, however, continues through Fernie another 3 hours or more to the Morrissey bridge. This stretch has more riffles and tends to be closer to the highway as the river gradually flows into an area more heavily timbered with evergreens.

Land along the Elk River is a confusing mix of private and federal ownership. (Federal lands are called "crown lands" in Canada.) Maps accurately showing public land have not been readily available, thus camping along the river is not recommended. Developed camping is available at Mount Fernie Provincial Park, 1.2 miles southwest of Fernie off Highway 3.

31 • Creston Valley Wildlife Area

Distance	•	19 miles
Time	•	10 hours or overnight
Season	•	Generally April through October
Shuttle	•	19 miles, pavement
Rating	•	Flatwater
Hazards	•	Powerboats on river; winds; hunting in fall
Information	•	Creston Valley Wildlife Interpretive Centre; Summit Creek Campground near Creston
Maps	•	Canada EMR Creston 82/F2, plus Creston Valley Wildlife Area map

Like those in uncounted other river valleys, the vast wetlands of the Creston Valley were nearly lost to development and agriculture. A conservation project initiated by sportsmen made the difference, and led to creation of the 17,000-acre Creston Valley Wildlife Area in 1968.

Dikes built to hold water into this area attract ducks, geese, and swans, though in much smaller numbers than before man tampered with the Kootenay River upstream and down. Biologists have counted more than 260 species of birds, with the greatest concentrations during the spring and fall migrations. Ospreys nest in the cottonwoods that line the river. Autumn visitors sometimes hear Rocky Mountain elk bugling from the tules. Kokanee salmon spawn in many of the creeks that feed the Kootenay.

The trip described here takes boaters from the meandering Kootenay River Channel—a quiet slough that was once the main river bed—to the Kootenay itself. It can be divided into two days, with a side trip up Summit Creek to the refuge campground. Many variations are possible. Although the river can be paddled year-round, other waters in the refuge freeze in winter. Summit Creek can be too low for paddling even when there is ample water elsewhere. Spring and fall are the best times to see wildlife.

Leisure paddling at Creston Valley Wildlife Area (Dan Hansen photo)

ACCESS

To reach the put-in from the town of Creston, British Columbia, drive west about 5 miles on Highway 3, crossing the Kootenay River, Nick's Island, and the old river channel before turning left on West Creston Road. The road comes to the slough a little more than 4 miles from the highway.

To reach the take-out, drive north from Creston on Highway 3A, passing through the villages of Wynndel and Sirdar. Fifteen miles from Creston, at the north end of Duck Lake, the road starts downhill. Near the bottom of the hill, turn left onto the first gravel road, which is a public access to the wildlife area. The road is gated a short distance from the highway.

PADDLE ROUTE

Immediately after launching at the put-in and crossing under the West Creston Road bridge, paddlers must decide whether they will follow the old river channel or the river itself. The channel, which leads to the left, is by far the more interesting of the two, providing the best views of wildlife and moderate shelter from the wind. But by late summer, it can be shallow and weed-choked. In that case, paddlers must bear right, crossing under another bridge and into the broad river, where boaters and skiers can be a nuisance on summer weekends and the wind can be ferocious.

From the put-in, the channel winds a lazy 6 miles to its confluence with Summit Creek. Boaters who are making the trip in two days should turn left at the creek, paddling upstream about a mile to a sandbar where the water becomes shallow and the current is strong. A rough road on the left leads from the creek to the Summit Creek Campground. Both the campground and Creston Valley Wildlife Interpretive Centre are open late-April through mid-October, although the waters of the management area are never closed. The tidy campground features hot showers and 300-year-old cedar trees. Several trails start here. By road, the campground is reached via Highway 3. Signs mark the route.

If the campground is not a destination, paddlers leaving the old river channel should follow Summit Creek downstream 2 miles to the main stem of the Kootenay River. The riverbanks are too steep and brushy in most places to provide easy landing or views of the surrounding lowlands.

About 5 miles downstream from Summit Creek, the river splits, and boaters should turn right onto the East Branch of the Kootenay. In another 3 miles, it is possible to climb the dike on the right side of

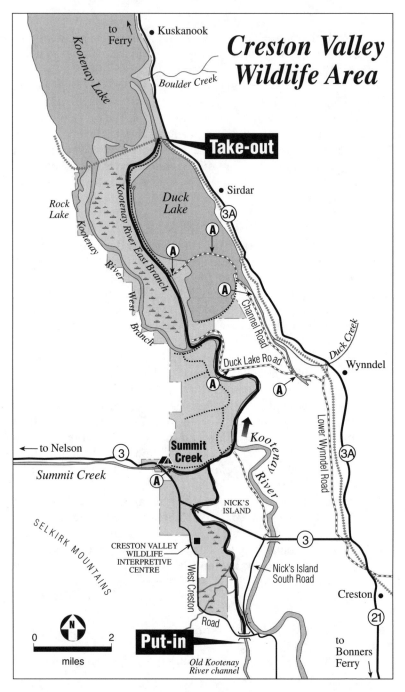

Creston Valley Wildlife Area

the river and look down into 3,000-acre Duck Lake. The take-out, 6 miles after the river splits, is about 100 yards upstream from the Canadian Pacific Railroad bridge at the north end of Duck Lake. Boaters should watch carefully for the overflow pipe from Duck Lake on the right side of the river. A rough trail leads to the top of the dike, and it's a quarter-mile carry from the take-out to the parking area.

Several trip options are possible. Paddlers with an extra day can launch just south of the Porthill border crossing and paddle about 12 miles on the Kootenay before reaching the put-in described above. For an even longer trip, paddlers can take the West Branch of the Kootenay, which leads to the remote western shore of Kootenay Lake, where there are several campgrounds accessible only by boat.

The trip can be turned into a week-long adventure by following the shoreline to the lake's west arm, which leads to the resort town of Nelson. Boaters who venture onto Kootenay Lake should use extreme caution, since winds can turn back even large vessels. Every trip schedule should include an extra day or two, in case the wind forces paddlers off the water.

Families, or boaters pinched for time, can enjoy peaceful paddling on Duck Lake, which sports good bass fishing and is off-limits to powerboats. The lake is a favorite nesting site for waterfowl, including five species of grebes, which perform elaborate spring courtship dances.

Naturalists lead hour-long guided canoe trips through the marshes at the interpretive center on West Creston Road.

IDAHO

32 • Moyie River

Distance	•	12 miles
Time	•	4 hours
Season	•	Generally June through early July
Shuttle	•	10 miles, pavement and gravel
Rating	•	Class 1
Hazards	•	Scattered rapids; rock gardens at low flows
Information	•	Bonners Ferry Ranger Station
Maps	•	USGS Eastport, Meadow Creek, plus Kaniksu National Forest map

The Moyie is a classic mountain stream: cold, clear, shallow, and shaded with cedars and cottonwoods. Ospreys dive into its pools for cutthroat and hatchery-reared rainbow trout. Deer, elk, and other large mammals live along its banks.

Born in the Purcell Mountains of British Columbia, the Moyie flows 58 miles in Canada and another 26 in Idaho before dumping into the larger Kootenai River about 10 miles east of Bonners Ferry. Moyie Falls Dam holds back the river a few miles from the Kootenai. The spectacular gorge below the dam, which can be seen from U.S. Highway 2, is the view most people have of the river.

This trip starts a mile south of the Canada border and follows the river about 12 shady miles. The leisurely half-day trip is interspersed with rapids that can reach Class 2 at high water. Boaters will scrape and bounce through innumerable rock gardens when the flow is much

less than 500 cubic feet per second. Camping is available at the put-in and 4 miles downstream from the take-out at the Meadow Creek Campground.

Moyie River (Dan Hansen photo)

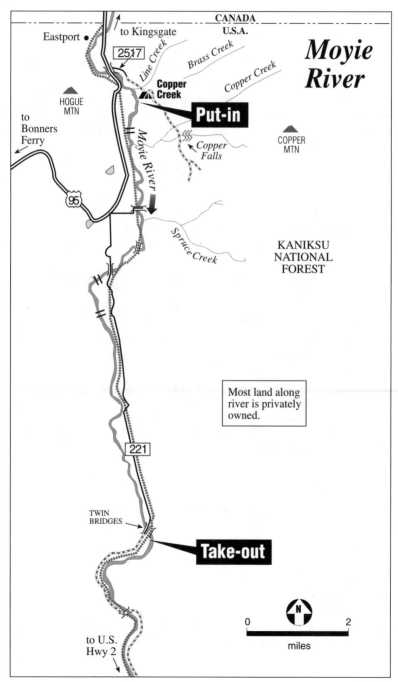

ACCESS

To reach the put-in from Bonners Ferry, drive north about 30 miles on U.S. Highway 95. Turn right onto Forest Service Road 2517, a gravel road that leads about a mile to Copper Creek Campground. A short carry leads to the river.

To reach the take-out from Copper Creek, drive 3 miles south on Highway 95 to Meadow Creek Road (Forest Service Road 221). Follow Meadow Creek Road 6 miles to Twin Bridges, where the paved road becomes gravel. There is a good take-out on the south side of the river, between the bridge for cars and its companion for trains.

PADDLE ROUTE

Flow information • USGS Water Resources in Sandpoint
River gauge • 12306500 near Eastport
Historic flows • Average 688; maximum 8,930; minimum 30

Below Twin Bridges the river gets progressively more technical, with Class 2-plus whitewater in the 7 miles between the bridges and Meadow Creek Campground. Beginning and intermediate paddlers should end their trip at the bridges. By no means should they go beyond the campground, where the river becomes a playground for experienced whitewater paddlers.

The U.S. Forest Service held a series of meetings in 1975 to consider protecting the Moyie under the Wild and Scenic River Act. Opposition from landowners was overwhelming, and the river remains unprotected. Nearly all shoreline along this trip is private, and is dotted with cabins, houses, and "for sale" signs. So far, the development does not detract from the journey.

33 • Upper Priest Lake

Distance • 7 miles round trip
Time • 4 hours or overnight
Season • Generally May through November
Shuttle • None
Rating • Flatwater
Hazards • Wind; occasional law-breaking powerboaters
Information • Priest Lake Ranger Station near Nordman
Maps • USGS Priest Lake NE, Caribou Creek, Upper Priest Lake, plus Kaniksu National Forest map

Flatwater morning on Upper Priest Lake (Rich Landers photo)

Numerous options make this trip suitable for anyone from power paddlers to families heading for a daytrip or campout at a North Idaho gem. By land, access to Upper Priest Lake is limited to muscle power. No roads lead to the 3.5-mile-long lake; no private development is allowed. This has left the lakeshore virtually pristine.

Unfortunately, the commotion of the larger Priest Lake creeps into Upper Priest because powerboats are allowed to motor up the 3-mile Thorofare separating the two lakes. Ironically, powerboaters flock to the upper lake on summer weekends to escape the madness on the big lake. Without restrictions on powerboats, the upper lake will ultimately be inundated with the noise, speed, and parties that plague other boating waters.

Meanwhile, Upper Priest Lake continues to be a premier paddling destination. Go in late spring and early fall for the best shot at solitude. During summer, the most pleasant paddling is on weekdays. But even on weekends, canoeists and kayakers can find themselves alone in paradise by paddling early in the morning and late in the day, when powerboat traffic is mostly gone.

Heavy flow down The Thorofare from Upper Priest during runoff periods in April and May can make upstream paddling difficult. By late June, flows are barely perceptible.

ACCESS

From Priest River, Idaho, drive 37 miles north on State Highway 57 to Nordman. Bear right onto paved Forest Road 1339 toward Reeder Bay. Pass Reeder Bay Campground. From the Ledgewood picnic area, where the road number changes to 2512, continue nearly 2 miles and turn into the Forest Service campground at Beaver Creek. Follow the signs to the boat launch, or skirt the north side of the camping area, continuing straight toward the lake and the day-use parking area.

As you drive into the Beaver Creek day-use area, watch for a sign on the left indicating the trailhead for the Lakeshore Trail and a quarter-mile portage trail that leads to The Thorofare. The trail is a good option should high winds develop and make the open water of Priest Lake dangerous to paddle.

This trip also can begin at Lions Head Campground, accessible from the east side of Priest Lake. From Highway 57 at the south end of Priest Lake, turn east at Dickensheet Junction. Go to Coolin, then drive about 24 miles north on East Shore Road. The last few miles to the campground are gravel. The campground, managed by Priest Lake State Park, is less developed than others around the lake. RV's are discouraged by small sites and no power hookups.

PADDLE ROUTE

From the boat launch or from the sandy beach at Beaver Creek, paddle around the point toward the north end of Priest Lake. If the water is calm, set your sights on the right (east) end of the wooden breakwater fence in the distance. Turn left around the end of the breakwater pilings. The water is shallow with a sand bottom here in Mosquito Bay. Paddle westward parallel to the fence. (Note: Should rough water arise unexpectedly, you can portage 100 feet over a sand spit at the west end of the wooden breakwater fence.) Continue west, paddling through a short gauntlet of private homes and into the entrance of The Thorofare. Here, development ends.

The Thorofare, generally protected by wind, adds a river-like feeling to this flatwater trip. Powerboats are supposed to go up The Thorofare at no-wake speed. The narrow waterway is lined with brush and trees, offering only a few spots to comfortably pull onto shore. At summer levels, however, you can find numerous mud bars. The first place to get out and really stretch muscles is at the beach in front of

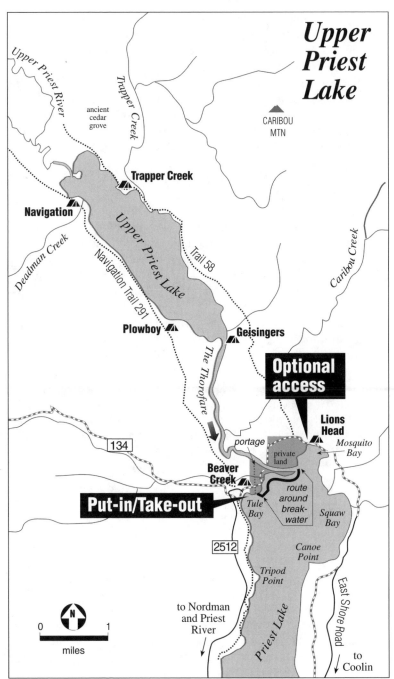

Upper Priest Lake

Upper Priest River

ancient cedar grove

Trapper Creek

CARIBOU MTN

Trapper Creek

Navigation

Deadman Creek

Upper Priest Lake

Navigation Trail 291

Trail 58

Caribou Creek

Plowboy

Geisingers

The Thorofare

Optional access

Lions Head

Mosquito Bay

134

portage

private land

Beaver Creek

route around break-water

Squaw Bay

Put-in/Take-out

Tule Bay

Canoe Point

2512

Tripod Point

to Nordman and Priest River

East Shore Road

Priest Lake

to Coolin

0   N   1

miles

Geisingers Campground at the outlet of Upper Priest Lake. Expect this popular campsite to be occupied.

The lake has three other pleasant semi-developed Forest Service campgrounds with outhouses. About ten undeveloped campsites have been hacked out along a shoreline that is generally too steep for camping. These sites, mostly on the east shore, range from solo-tent size to expansive enough for several tents. Sanitation can be a problem at these sites, since the steep terrain discourages some people from going as far from camp as they should for personal latrines. Upper Priest Lake is gin-clear, but bring your home-filled containers, or be equipped with purification devices, as water from the lake or streams should always be treated before consumption.

The lake offers good options for hiking. Campgrounds at the west side of Upper Priest provide access to explore the shoreline on Navigation Trail 291. From Geisingers Campground, you can hook up with an old road, closed to motor vehicles, that leads back to Lions Head Campground. The Trapper Creek campground gives access to a trail that leads northwest along the lakeshore, past an old cabin, and north to a forest of ancient cedars. If you prefer to do your exploring by boat, paddle to the northwest end of the lake and poke upstream as far as you can into the Upper Priest River.

Upper Priest Lake is in a Panhandle National Forests scenic area somewhat protected from chainsaws. The Salmo-Priest Wilderness lies to the northwest. The watershed is home to a who's who of the region's endangered species, including mountain caribou, wolves, grizzly bears, and bull trout. Mycologists know the area for its abundance and variety of mushrooms: more than 1,000 documented species.

A contact useful for boaters is Priest Lake State Park.

34 · Priest River

Distance	•	28 miles
Time	•	12 hours or overnight
Season	•	Generally May through June or October
Shuttle	•	26 miles, pavement
Rating	•	Class 1, with one Class 2 rapid
Hazards	•	Downed trees
Information	•	Priest Lake Ranger Station near Nordman
Maps	•	USGS Coolin, Outlet Bay, Prater Mountain, plus Kaniksu National Forest map

Autumn on Priest River (Dan Hansen photo)

Priest Lake is the jewel of North Idaho, set amid cedar and pine forests at the base of the craggy Selkirk crest. But while the lake is lined with cabins and resorts, and powerboats crisscross in every direction over its surface, the river that flows from the lake provides quiet paddling. Most land to the west of the Priest River is managed by the U.S. Forest Service; most on the east is the Priest Lake State Forest. While both the state and federal governments lease land for cabins along the lake, development along the river is limited to pockets of private land.

Autumn is prime time on the river. Each year, typically starting mid-October, Avista Utilities Company begins drawing down Priest Lake to make room for runoff that will refill the lake six months later. Water spills over Outlet Dam and into the river, creating ideal paddling just as fall colors peak. The mosquitoes are gone, as are most tourists. Fall visitors may spot beavers that build dams on many of the creeks flowing into the river, or wood ducks that thrive on the ponds.

The draw-down does not always occur like clockwork, and paddlers should call WWP before committing to a trip.

Priest River flows 44 miles from Priest Lake to its confluence with the Pend Oreille River. The section described here is 28 miles long, with the option of cutting 10 miles off the trip.

ACCESS

Those planning an overnight trip should leave a vehicle at the McAbee Falls take-out before driving to the put-in at Dickensheet Campground. To reach McAbee, drive north on State Highway 57 from the town of Priest River, Idaho. Turn right at 3.5 miles, and follow Peninsula Road about 5 miles to the river. Misnamed McAbee Falls is a Class 1-plus rapid that starts under the bridge.

To reach the put-in, drive north on Highway 57 an additional 20 miles past Peninsula Road. Turn right at Dickensheet Junction, onto Coolin Road. In less than a mile, Coolin Road crosses the Priest River at state-owned Dickensheet Campground. Boaters can park in the campground, within a few feet of the river.

For a single day on the river, paddlers should launch at Dickensheet Campground and take out 18 miles downstream at a spot called Big Hole.

To reach Big Hole, follow Peninsula Road until just before McAbee Falls, then turn west onto Forest Service Road 334. This dirt road, which is rough in places, weaves through the forest on the west side of the river, coming into sight of the water only occasionally. About 7 miles from Peninsula Road, a big bend in the river is visible from the road. There is room to park a car or two. A faint and steep trail leads about 100 yards to the river. (Drivers who miss this take-out will come to a cluster of houses in about a mile.) Two miles past Big Hole, Road 334 joins Forest Service Road 239. Highway 57 is another 5 miles beyond the junction, and from there it is 4.5 miles to Dickensheet Junction.

Hike to the river at Big Hole before starting a trip. Note a few landmarks at this take-out, which is as easy to miss from the water as it is from the road.

PADDLE ROUTE

Flow information • Avista Utilities or USGS Water Resources in Sandpoint

River gauge • 12395000 near the town of Priest River

Historic flows • Average 1,503; maximum 10,400; minimum 191

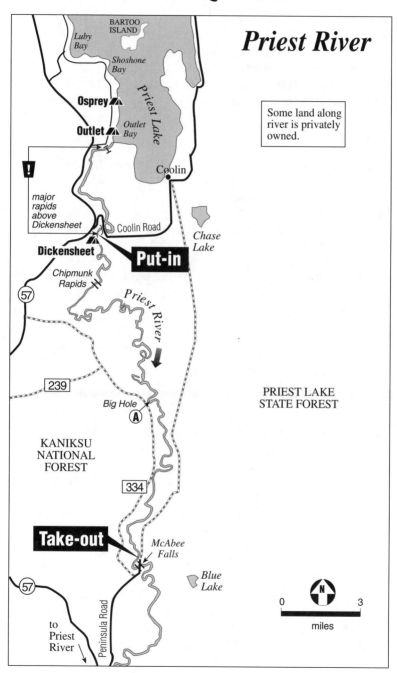

Priest River

Some land along river is privately owned.

BARTOO ISLAND

Luby Bay

Shoshone Bay

Priest Lake

Osprey

Outlet

Outlet Bay

Coolin

major rapids above Dickensheet

Coolin Road

Chase Lake

Dickensheet

Put-in

Chipmunk Rapids

57

Priest River

239

PRIEST LAKE STATE FOREST

Big Hole
A

KANIKSU NATIONAL FOREST

334

Take-out

McAbee Falls

Blue Lake

57

Peninsula Road

to Priest River

N

0   3
miles

Chipmunk Rapids, about 3 miles downstream from Dickensheet, is the only significant whitewater of the trip. Little maneuvering is required, and the rapids should not pose a problem for intermediate paddlers. About 10 miles into the trip, the river begins a series of oxbows in a broad valley of private grazing land. Boaters will pass perhaps a dozen houses, cabins, and shacks before once again coming into public forest. Downstream from Big Hole, the river is mostly flat and meandering.

Several good campsites are downstream from Chipmunk Rapids, but campers must pay close attention to the Forest Service map to assure that they are on public, rather than private, land.

In the early twentieth century, the Priest River gained fame among anglers as the place to fill a creel with native cutthroat trout. Eastern dudes with split bamboo fly rods fished beside settlers with willow rods. Logging has filled the stream with silt. The decline was furthered by Outlet Dam, which controls the flow of water from Priest Lake and causes the river to run low and warm in summer. Although the Priest still has the look of a prime trout stream, it holds few fish.

35 · Pack River

Distance	•	22.5 miles
Time	•	8–12 hours
Season	•	Generally April through October
Shuttle	•	14 miles, pavement
Rating	•	Class 1 and flatwater
Hazards	•	Tight turns; strainers, logjams; wind at Pack River Flats
Information	•	Pack River General Store northeast of Sandpoint
Maps	•	USGS Colburn, Elmira, Oden Bay, Trout Peak, plus Kaniksu National Forest map

The Pack River begins in northern Idaho's best alpine scenery along the crest of the Selkirk Mountains near Chimney Rock and Harrison Peak. It flows 45 miles before unloading into Lake Pend Oreille, one of Idaho's world-class freshwater destinations. Along the way, humans have left some disappointing clearcuts and ill-advised roads. The small native cutthroat trout found high in the watershed do not do well lower in the drainage. But paddlers can find some wild moments.

The upper river, which starts in the Kaniksu National Forest, is narrow and swift. Skilled kayakers can find room to play in portions of the upper river when the flows are sufficient. Lower in the drainage, where the river becomes tame enough for average canoeists, most of the shoreline is privately owned. By putting in at bridges off Pack River Road, paddlers can find lively water roughly from Tavern Creek downstream to Highway 95. That section usually has enough water for paddling in June, but the flows can become too low in July. Be aware that the river upstream from Highway 95 has some tight turns that are prone to dangerous logjams.

The river from Highway 95 downstream to the mouth is the most accommodating to paddlers, offering several options for customizing the length of the trip. Paddle the entire 22.5 miles, or break it up into half-day segments.

Golf course slough along Pack River (Rich Landers photo)

ACCESS

From the junction with State Highway 200 north of Sandpoint, drive north on U.S. Highway 2/95 nearly 10 miles to the put-in and unimproved parking area on the east side of the highway just north of the Pack River bridge (milepost 485.8).

To reach the take-out, backtrack south on Highway 2/95 about 2 miles. Turn east onto Colburn-Culver Road (milepost 483.7) and drive 6 miles (east then south) to a school. An optional take-out is at the bridge just before this school. To make this a 12.5-mile trip, go to the other optional take-out by turning left (east) at the school onto Rapid Lightning Creek Road. Drive 1.5 miles to a take-out on the east side of the Pack River bridge next to the fire station. Do not block the fire station driveway.

To reach the mouth of the Pack River, continue south from the school on Colburn-Culver Road for 2.8 miles to the junction with State Highway 200. (This junction is at milepost 36 for paddlers coming from Sandpoint on Highway 200.) Head east on the highway and drive 4.8 miles to a dirt road (milepost 40.8) that leads down from the highway to the shore at Pack River Flats near a railroad dike.

Other optional take-outs are at Highway 200 on the east side of the Pack River bridge (milepost 38.8) and at several pull-outs off Highway 200 along Pack River Flats.

PADDLE ROUTE

Flow information • USGS stopped gauge readings near
Colburn in 1992

Historic flows • Average not available; maximum 4,330;
minimum 36

This lazy, windy tour through forested meadows can be negotiated by paddlers with modest skills in a wide range of flow levels. The trip goes quickly with higher flows in May and June. Lower flows can make for a long day. Although surrounding land is mostly private, sand and gravel bars offer options for stopping, swimming, or picnicking below the high water mark. The trip offers a good chance of seeing wildlife, including beavers, bald eagles, ospreys, moose, deer, wood ducks, and spotted sandpipers bobbing their tails along shore.

Once under the railroad trestle from the put-in, paddlers enter what is, although short, the wildest stretch of this trip. In the first 2 miles, the river bends around a forested knob. Cedars lean over the water. The conifer forest gradually gives way to cottonwood bottoms under attack by beavers. Cabins and homes crop up increasingly along the river, but detract little from the experience.

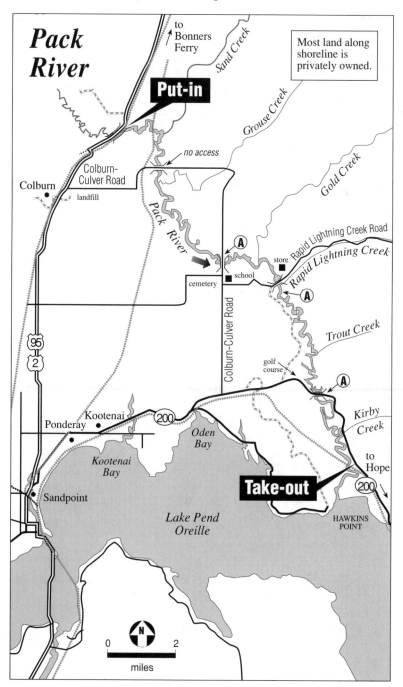

Pack River

to Bonners Ferry

Put-in

no access

Colburn-Culver Road

Colburn

landfill

Most land along shoreline is privately owned.

Sand Creek

Grouse Creek

Gold Creek

Pack River

Ⓐ

Rapid Lightning Creek Road

store

Rapid Lightning Creek

cemetery

school

Ⓐ

Trout Creek

golf course

Ⓐ

Kirby Creek

Kootenai

Ponderay

200

Oden Bay

Take-out

to Hope

200

Kootenai Bay

HAWKINS POINT

Sandpoint

Lake Pend Oreille

0   N   2

miles

Float 3.7 miles to the first Colburn-Culver Road bridge, where there is no easy or legal access. After a long straight stretch downstream from the bridge, the river meanders become very tight. Paddle past one side of a house; 10 minutes later, you paddle past the other side of the same house. Pass the optional access at the second Colburn-Culver Road bridge 9.8 miles from the start. The lazy nature of the stream can lull paddlers. Always watch ahead for obstructions.

From the Rapid Lightning Road bridge, another good access, paddlers drift into prime moose country and past several sloughs worth investigating for waterfowl, ospreys, and other creatures. Cattle grazing is more apparent. In midsummer, sandbars can be wide and grass tall along the banks. Hidden in the brush are the mouths of tributary streams, including Trout Creek.

A rough, rocky take-out is at the Highway 200 bridge. But the nearly 4 miles of flatwater paddling through Pack River Flats is pleasant, with a good chance of seeing more birds and wildlife. Paddlers generally can follow the river channel, or blaze a trail over the flats, which are flooded when the level of Lake Pend Oreille is high. Scout the flats from the road when shuttling cars.

36 • Clark Fork River Delta

Distance	•	7 miles round trip
Time	•	4–6 hours
Season	•	Virtually year-round
Shuttle	•	None
Rating	•	Flatwater with some upstream paddling
Hazards	•	Deadheads; paddling upstream against stiff current in high flows; wind off Lake Pend Oreille
Information	•	Sandpoint Chamber of Commerce
Maps	•	USGS Clark Fork

Sea kayakers and canoeists alike will enjoy this loop tour with its fascinating combination of flowing and still waters at the northeast end of Lake Pend Oreille. After surging out of Cabinet Gorge Dam, the river eventually braids into three branches called the North, Middle, and South Forks. The route described here has several shorter options or variations through these forks in an area informally managed as the Pend Oreille State Wildlife Management Area.

Attractions include the numerous undeveloped islands, and coves and inlets left as havens for a wide range of wildlife—including deer, mink, ospreys, bald eagles, waterfowl, and numerous songbirds. Fall foliage is an attraction in itself.

ACCESS

From Sandpoint, Idaho, drive 25 miles east on State Highway 200 to the town of Clark Fork (milepost 55). At the east end of Clark Fork, turn south on Stevens Road. Cross the railroad tracks and bear left on the paved road. Immediately after crossing a one-lane bridge, turn right. Drive 2.5 miles on the dirt road. At the Y with Forest Service Road 278, bear right to get to the put-in at Johnson Creek access.

PADDLE ROUTE

Flow information   •   Cabinet Gorge Dam
Historic flows   •   Average 22,410; maximum 153,000; minimum 3,000

Be prepared for changing conditions. Water levels on this route are affected down-lake by Albeni Falls Dam, which can cause Lake Pend Oreille to fluctuate up to 11 feet during the year. The Clark Fork River

Exploring a slough in Clark Fork River Delta (Rich Landers photo)

is controlled by several upstream dams, including Cabinet Gorge, built in 1952. In midsummer, the dam can shut down to minimum allowable flows of 3,000 cfs—plenty low enough to make portions of this route shallow and rocky, especially near two bridges at the upstream entrance to the South Fork. The minimum flows typically occur at night, when there is less demand for power. Scout the river channel from the road on the way to the put-in.

Some paddlers will shrug off low water as a good excuse to climb out of the boat and use fishing rods, since the waters hold trout, bass, and squawfish.

Follow the recommended route clockwise, heading downstream from the put-in. A rock beach at the mouth of the South Fork is a good picnic spot or campsite. If big winds develop, simply turn tail back into the protected waters of the South Fork.

The rest of the route is fairly easy, depending on your paddling skills, wind conditions, and river flows. For instance, on a typical June day, the flow of the Clark Fork River out of Cabinet Gorge Dam can be 33,000 cubic feet per second at noon, providing significant but not overwhelming current in the South Fork. By 5:00 P.M., the river flow out of the dam may increase to 52,000 cfs, leaving the South Fork still reasonably easy to negotiate upstream. However, some paddlers might have difficulty navigating those flows against the stronger current in the upper Middle Fork.

The map shows one of several possible alternate routes to shorten the trip and avoid the Middle Fork.

When Albeni Falls Dam went on line in 1955, much of the Clark Fork Delta area was purchased by the U.S. Army Corps of Engineers and turned over to the Idaho Fish and Game Department. However, portions of Derr Island and most of the islands west of the river mouth are private land. This route passes numerous hidden coves worth exploring, plus goose nesting platforms usually occupied in early May.

Pilings in the Middle Fork are designed to divert logs and other river debris to a drift yard at the end of the North Fork upstream from Hope. The drift yard is part of a project funded by Albeni Falls that collects about 10 acres of driftwood each year and prevents it from floating into Lake Pend Oreille.

Sightseers can follow the access road upstream to Cabinet Gorge Fish Hatchery. The hatchery normally is open to visitors during the day. The main attraction is in late fall, when returning kokanee are captured and stripped of eggs for propagation. Guided canoe and sea kayaking trips may be offered in this area; contact the Sandpoint Chamber of Commerce for information.

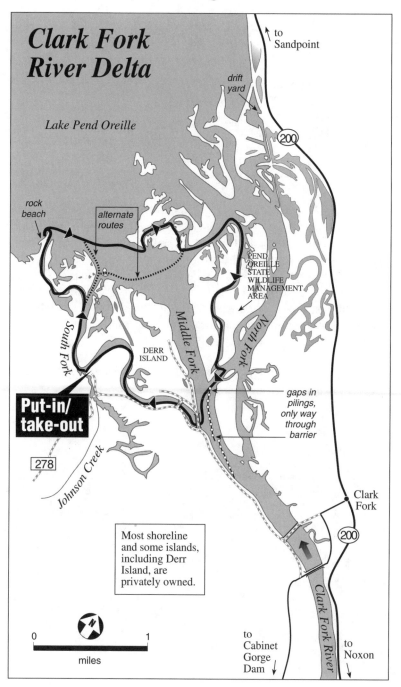

Clark Fork River Delta

to Sandpoint

drift yard

200

Lake Pend Oreille

rock beach

alternate routes

PEND OREILLE STATE WILDLIFE MANAGEMENT AREA

South Fork

Middle Fork

North Fork

DERR ISLAND

gaps in pilings, only way through barrier

Put-in/ take-out

278

Johnson Creek

Clark Fork

200

Most shoreline and some islands, including Derr Island, are privately owned.

0 ——————— 1
miles

to Cabinet Gorge Dam

Clark Fork River

to Noxon

37 • Coeur d'Alene River

Distance	•	9.5 miles
Time	•	1.5–3 hours
Season	•	Virtually year-round
Shuttle	•	7 miles, pavement
Rating	•	Class 1; some Class 2 possible
Hazards	•	Some sharp bends; strainers
Information	•	Enaville Resort at Enaville
Maps	•	USGS Cataldo; plus Coeur d'Alene National Forest map

Drifting down the clear water, along the timbered shores of this stretch, a paddler might find it hard to imagine the dichotomies that history has brought together in the Coeur d'Alene River: native cutthroat trout against insensitive logging and mining; the long-gone Snakepit brothel at Enaville against the still-standing Jesuit Indian mission near Cataldo. Legacies good and bad live here. Be sure to visit Old Mission State Park, but don't swim or play in the dirt at the Mission Flats take-out. The area is contaminated with heavy metals from a century of Silver Valley mining.

February on Coeur d'Alene River near Cataldo (Rich Landers photo)

Flows in this section of the Coeur d'Alene River typically are high enough for paddling most of the year. Exceptions to the rule include low flows during occasional weeks of extreme cold temperatures in winter and dry weather in late August or September. Also, the brief period of winter or spring flooding makes the river unsafe. Normally, however, the river gets a Class 1 rating, with no serious rapids.

The river from Enaville to Cataldo generally parallels roads, but swings away for decent stretches of solitude. It holds some splashy riffles for play, plus a few tight turns to test paddling skills. The water is clear most of the year, with the bottom visible even in deeper holes. Most bridges are festooned with swinging ropes. The area is prized for native cutthroat trout, although they have not held their own against man's tinkering in this drainage. The Idaho Fish and Game Department also has stocked rainbow trout for anglers in this stretch.

The river begins near the divide that separates the drainage from Lake Pend Oreille. It flows 113 miles, collecting more water from the North Fork and South Fork before emptying into Lake Coeur d'Alene at Harrison, Idaho.

ACCESS

To reach the take-out from Interstate 90 between Coeur d'Alene and Kellogg, Idaho, take exit 39 toward Old Mission State Park. Go nearly a mile, following the frontage road paralleling I-90, past the historic mission, to the Mission Flats boat ramp.

To reach the put-in from the Old Mission Park exit, drive east on I-90 about 4 miles and turn off on Kingston exit 43. Head north on Coeur d'Alene River Road, pass Enaville Resort, and be prepared to turn right on Old River Road at 2 miles from I-90. Bear left at the Y and cross the bridge over the Coeur d'Alene River. The put-in is near a tavern. Paddlers who leave vehicles on or near private property should always ask permission and get directions to preferred parking areas.

PADDLE ROUTE

Flow information • USGS Water Resources in Sandpoint
River gauge • 12413500 at Cataldo
Historic flows • Average 2,499; maximum 50,000; minimum 141

This stretch of the river is popular with swimmers and floating vessels of all types on hot summer weekends, but is virtually unused from fall through spring. Notable tricky spots include the standing waves and a sudden turn just after the river bends north away from Coeur d'Alene

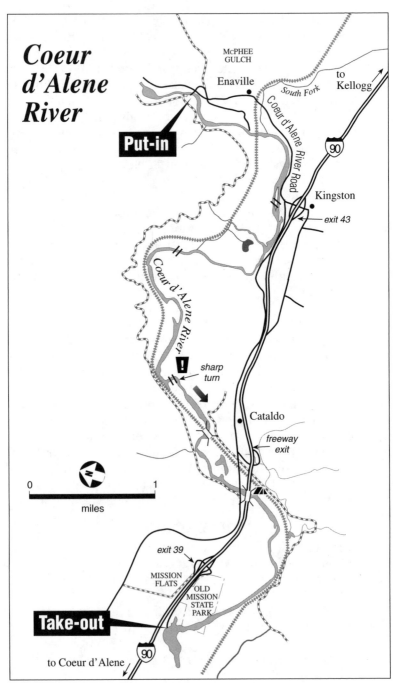

Coeur d'Alene River

McPHEE GULCH

Enaville

South Fork

to Kellogg

Put-in

Coeur d'Alene River Road

90

Kingston

exit 43

Coeur d'Alene River

! sharp turn

Cataldo

freeway exit

0   1
miles

exit 39

MISSION FLATS

OLD MISSION STATE PARK

Take-out

90

to Coeur d'Alene

River Road. Also be on guard for the turbulence at a rock wall where the river turns 90° to the right, shortly before flowing under I-90. This spot is easily avoided with a short portage if desired.

The last straight stretch to the Mission Flats take-out moves slowly, since it's on the verge of slack water backed up from Lake Coeur d'Alene.

The river's worst floods have been caused by rain-on-snow events during winter; for example 79,000 cubic feet per second during the flood of 1974 and 40,000 cfs during floods in 1996 and 1997. However, high average runoff tends to be around 7,000 cfs at Enaville for about two weeks between late April and early June. The lowest average flows tend to be around 145 cfs in August or September. Floating the river is a no-brainer at 2,500 to 3,500 cfs.

To extend this trip by about 5 miles, drive north on the Coeur d'Alene River Road to the turnoff to Bumblebee Campground. After crossing the bridge over the river, drive downstream, looking for undeveloped access points. The river offers good paddling farther upstream, almost to the confluence with Tepee Creek, when flows are adequate. The river is tighter and more technical in its upper stretches, as well as more susceptible to logjams. By sometime in July, the river gets too low for floating above Shoshone Creek.

This trip includes plenty of gravel beaches for stopping and picnicking. Although most surrounding land is managed by the Panhandle National Forests, much of it is privately owned. Several Forest Service campgrounds are along the river upstream from Prichard, where Babin's Store sells fishing licenses, groceries, and gas.

38 • Lower Coeur d'Alene River

Distance •	At least 16 miles
Time •	1 long day or overnight
Season •	Generally March through December
Shuttle •	30 miles, pavement
Rating •	Flatwater
Hazards •	Powerboats; deadheads; wind; soil contamination from mine waste; hunting
Information •	Panhandle National Forests; Bureau of Land Management; Idaho Fish and Game; all in Coeur d'Alene
Maps •	USGS Lane, Medimont, Black Lake, Harrison, plus Coeur d'Alene National Forest map

Swarms of perch, crappie, and bass easily support predators that hunt this area from the air and underwater, as well as from boats. Ospreys, great blue herons, and waterfowl, including grebes and good numbers of wood ducks, are your constant companions on this grand sprawl of lakes and marshlands along the lower Coeur d'Alene River. Toothy northern pike lurk in the weedy shallows.

Osprey with lunch on Lower Coeur d'Alene River
(Rich Landers photo)

The river channel is flanked by numerous wetlands and eight lakes that boaters can reach through narrow causeways. Slack water from Lake Coeur d'Alene virtually eliminates current in the lower river for much of the year. Paddlers willing to apply muscle power can customize numerous variations of this trip for a rewarding fishing or wildlife-viewing experience. The area bustles with wild creatures, including mink, muskrats, beaver, and shorebirds. Tundra swans migrate through in spring and fall, with the largest concentrations in March.

Be warned, however, that waste from the Wallace-Kellogg mining districts in the Silver Valley has been washing downstream for a century to coat the floodplain. Do not allow children to play in the benign-looking sand along the shores. Soils here are contaminated with heavy metals, including lead and zinc. After spring runoff, the metals seem to lock into the lake-bottom sediment, leaving the water safe for swimming. Boating in this area or even occasional forays onto the shores are not likely to harm people who exercise reasonable caution.

The wildlife tell us that all is not well. Each spring, biologists find the carcasses of swans and other waterfowl dead from lead poisoning after consuming the roots of vegetation growing from the sediment.

ACCESS

To reach the put-in from Interstate 90 between Coeur d'Alene and Kellogg, Idaho, take exit 34 toward Rose Lake. Go south on State Highway 3 about 5 miles and turn right onto Killarney Lake Road. Drive 3.5 miles to the Killarney Lake boat launch and campground, managed by the U.S. Bureau of Land Management.

To reach the take-out, go back to Highway 3 and continue southwest about 17 miles to the junction with State Highway 97. Turn north and drive 7 miles to Harrison. The take-out is at the marina boat launch below the city park. Leave vehicles away from the resort area on a side street. Parking spaces are needed for the small town's businesses. It is only a short walk from the launch uphill to virtually anywhere in town.

Harrison is accessible from the south via Moscow and Highway 95. The take-out also can be reached from the north by turning off I-90 at Wolf Lodge exit 22 and driving a tedious 28 miles south on curvy Highway 97.

Use the Coeur d'Alene National Forest map for navigating to several other public access points along the lower Coeur d'Alene River, including:

- Rainy Hill Campground and boat launch, managed by Panhandle National Forests at Medimont off Highway 3.

- Black Lake Resort boat launch off Highway 3.
- Thompson Lake boat launch, managed by the Idaho Fish and Game Department, on Thompson Lake Road northeast of Harrison.

Other river accesses can be found upstream from Killarney Lake at the town of Rose Lake and at Cataldo Mission. But the river from Killarney to Cataldo Mission is fairly featureless. Incidentally, the mission boat access area was the turnaround point for wooden ferries that once hauled timber up the river for the Silver Valley mines.

PADDLE ROUTE

Lake level information	• Avista Utilities recording
Normal summer pool level	• 2,128 feet

The campground at 480-acre Killarney Lake is not inviting, as it shares tight quarters with the commotion of boat launching and parking. The first island north of the Killarney launch is largely private land, but farther north on the lake, Popcorn Island has a boat-in campsite with outhouses.

The first challenge for paddlers is finding the channel out of Killarney. The causeway is the largest of all the entries to the lakes along the river. But as you look southwest from the launch, the channel is hidden by a spit and expanses of tubular jointed vegetation standing tall like green stubble along the lakeshore. The dominant plant of the marshes is called *equisetum*, better known as horsetail. It has no food value for wildlife, but probably provides cover for waterfowl broods and warmwater fish. Look carefully across these marshes for the contrasting bright head of a great blue heron, the stealthy fish hunter of the waterways.

Idaho Fish and Game workers have planted wild rice, which flourishes in the marsh between Killarney and Hidden Lake. Waterfowl flock to the rice when the grain matures around the first of September.

Mileage for the tour described here begins at the Killarney launch and runs down the river. Paddlers can add miles and days to the trip, depending on how curious they are to explore the lateral lakes. After paddling from Killarney, turn west to head downstream on the Coeur d'Alene River. Points of interest include:

- *Rainy Hill boat launch and RV campground, 4 miles on river-left:* Watch for the causeway that leads under a railroad trestle and concrete road bridge to Medicine Lake, 170 acres. Bear right and paddle under a larger bridge to reach Cave Lake and the scattering of

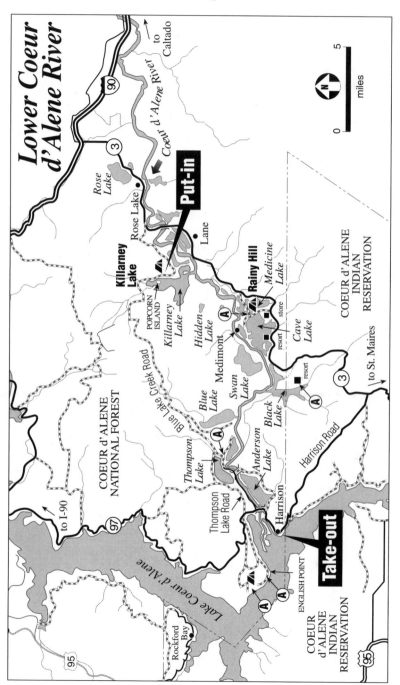

Lower Coeur d'Alene River

buildings called Medimont. At 600 acres, Cave is the largest of the lakes along the lower river. But it is shallow and loses much of its open water to weeds and marsh in summer. The lake has two resorts. (Note: entry under the first road bridge to Medicine and Cave Lakes hinges on the pool elevation of Lake Coeur d'Alene. At spring levels above 2,130 feet, clearance gets tight.)

- *Swan Lake, 6.5 miles on river-right:* The entrance to this 370-acre lake appears out of nowhere on a broad treeless flat. The lake, with its rugged, roadless north shore, is one of the most isolated along the river, accessible only by boat. A rocky peninsula, which can become an island in high water, is state land with an undeveloped campsite.

- *Black Lake, 8 miles on river-left:* Pass under a trestle, a favored swallow nest site, and up the causeway to the 350-acre lake, which has more homes than other lakes along the lower river. Water skiing is popular. Public access is at a resort on the south shore, reached from Black Lake Road off Highway 3.

- *Blue Lake, 10.5 miles on river-right:* Surrounded by timbered private land, this 200-acre lake has remained undeveloped. But it's a target for water-skiers.

- *Thompson Lake, 12.5 miles on river-right:* Pass a public boat launch as you head into this 400-acre lake, known for strict regulations to protect quality bass fishing. Some public land suitable for camping can be found on the lake's west arm, about half of which is marsh. Large floating islands can be found here, as well as stands of wild rice, which the Idaho Fish and Game Department leaves unharvested for the dining delight of waterfowl. From the boat access at the outlet, paddlers can walk through a cable gate to hike the dike road around Bare Marsh, a 200-acre wetland between Thompson and Blue Lakes.

- *Anderson Lake, 15 miles on river-left:* The outlet to this 400-acre lake is just upstream from the Highway 97 bridge over the Coeur d'Alene River. A road runs along the south shore.

- *Harrison, 16 miles at river mouth:* Buoys mark the river channel as it enters Lake Coeur d'Alene, but paddlers usually can take a shortcut through the shallow water, finding a direct route south to the marina at Harrison. Expect to see plenty of osprey activity here from spring through fall.

The best time to paddle along the lower Coeur d'Alene River during summer is early morning and late evening, when powerboat traffic is light and wildlife-viewing is more pleasant. Prime time is before spring runoff in March and early April as well as September and early October, when few recreational boaters are on the water, and waterfowl migrations are in full swing. The stretch with the most remote feeling is between Swan and Blue Lakes.

The public boat ramps at Cataldo Mission, Killarney, Rainy Hill, and Thompson are popular staging areas for waterfowl hunters from mid-October into December.

Patches of public land, mostly on the north shore of the river, offer camping, picnicking, and hiking opportunities. Many boaters camp along the shores of the river, although some are tenting on private property. The Coeur d'Alene National Forest map is the best guide to the ample but scattered public land along the river.

Fishing in these lakes can be excellent for largemouth and smallmouth bass, perch, crappie, bullheads, and northern pike. Fishing regulations vary among the lakes. The authors recommend that anglers avoid heavy consumption of fish caught in these waters, but Idaho health agencies have not been so bold.

39 • St. Joe–Three Lakes

Distance •	5 miles
Time •	2 hours
Season •	Generally March through November
Shuttle •	9 miles, pavement
Rating •	Flatwater
Hazards •	Wind; powerboats; waterfowl hunting in October and November
Information •	Heyburn State Park near Chatcolet
Maps •	USGS Benewah Lake, Black Lake, Chatcolet, Harrison, plus St. Joe National Forest map

A power plant on the Spokane River has created an unusual paddling experience 32 water miles away at the south end of Lake Coeur d'Alene. Construction of Post Falls Dam in 1906 backed water through Lake Coeur d'Alene and raised the level of Chatcolet Lake to merge it with Round and Benewah Lakes. However, the banks of the St. Joe are high enough to form a natural tree-lined levee that creates a river within the lakes.

Paddlers can enjoy an intimate visit with this final few miles of

what is known as the Shadowy St. Joe, because of the shade offered by the cottonwoods lining the river. The entire route is within Heyburn State Park, the first state park to be designated in Idaho. Heyburn, the second largest of Idaho's state parks, totals 7,825 acres; 2,333 acres are water.

ACCESS

This trip can be done in either direction. To reach the west access, drive east on State Highway 5 from Plummer, Idaho, for 6.5 miles and turn north onto the paved road toward Chatcolet. Go north 2.5 miles, passing Hawleys Landing Campground and Heyburn State Park headquarters, to a large boat launch and parking area.

To reach the east access, drive back to Highway 5. Continue east 5.3 miles and turn north at a sign toward Benewah Lake Campground. (If coming from St. Maries, the turnoff is between mileposts 11 and

"River within a lake" at St. Joe River mouth. Note tug towing rafts of logs. (Rich Landers photo)

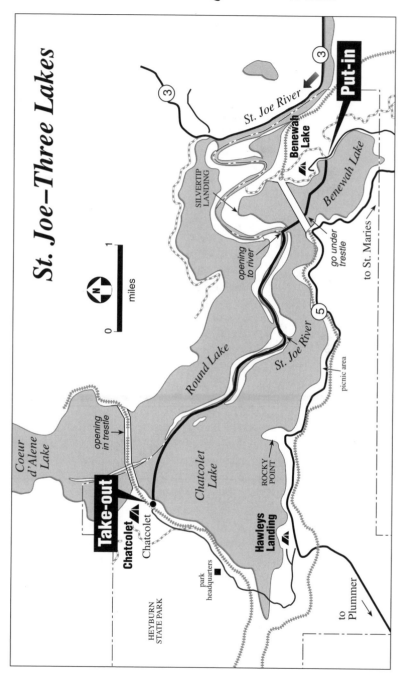

St. Joe–Three Lakes

Put-in

St. Joe River

Benewah Lake

Benewah Lake

SILVERTIP LANDING

opening to river

go under trestle

to St. Maries

N

miles

0   1

Round Lake

St. Joe River

picnic area

Coeur d'Alene Lake

opening in trestle

Chatcolet Lake

ROCKY POINT

Hawleys Landing

Take-out

Chatcolet

Chatcolet

park headquarters

HEYBURN STATE PARK

to Plummer

12.) Follow the paved road a mile to the resort, then bear left toward the campground. The boat launch is between the resort and the campground.

PADDLE ROUTE

Beginning from Benewah Lake, the route passes wild rice stands, then heads under a railroad trestle. Bear left along the cottonwood-studded banks of the St. Joe River. Look for an opening in the bank that allows access to the river channel. Beware of powerboats and the occasional tug towing a raft of logs bound for area mills. Follow the channel northwest. Boat houses at Rocky Point are a good landmark. The destination, however, is the next cluster of boat houses farther north at Chatcolet.

The St. Joe, elevation 2,125 feet at its mouth, is the world's highest navigable river, according to Idaho State Parks literature. Benewah Lake plus portions of Chatcolet and Round Lakes typically freeze by mid-December. Wild rice grows throughout marsh areas, where the harvest, done by air-boats, begins in early September.

The lakes, marshes, rice, and river attract a variety of songbirds, plus larger profile birds including herons, waterfowl, ospreys, and wild turkeys. Fish include bass, bluegills, crappies, perch, and squawfish, plus the occasional trout straying down from the cooler mountain waters of the upper St. Joe. Wildflowers are plentiful in spring.

Heyburn State Park is open year-round. Campgrounds, however, close late in November and reopen in April. Cabins are available at Benewah Lake Resort.

40 · St. Joe River

Distance	•	17 miles
Time	•	6 hours or overnight
Season	•	Generally June through mid-July
Shuttle	•	17 miles, mostly pavement
Rating	•	Class 2 above Marble Creek, Class 1 below
Hazards	•	Strainers, scattered rapids
Information	•	Avery Ranger Station near Avery
Maps	•	USGS Wallace SE, Wallace SW, Calder SE, Calder SW, plus St. Joe National Forest map

St. Joe River near Huckleberry Campground (Steve Thompson photo)

Anyone who reads national fly-fishing magazines has heard of the St. Joe River. Cars with license plates from around the nation can be spotted at dusty pull-outs along the upper river. From those rigs step anglers who search the river for wild westslope cutthroat trout.

While the catch-and-release fishing can be spectacular, it is not the only attraction on the St. Joe. Flowing 134 miles from the Bitterroot crest to Lake Coeur d'Alene, the river offers nearly every style of boating imaginable. Tour boats, ski boats, and tugs ply the slow, broad expanses near the river's mouth, while whitewater kayakers ride Class 4 waves near its mountainous source. Between are many miles of river suitable for casual paddlers.

This trip explores 17 miles of water starting at the Avery Ranger Station, about 6 miles downstream from the town of Avery. The trip can be shortened by using either of two alternative accesses. One eliminates most of the whitewater.

ACCESS

Boaters going the entire distance should leave a car in Calder, Idaho. From St. Maries, drive north on State Highway 3 to the St. Joe River Road (Forest Service Highway 50). At 23 miles, turn left on Calder Road, which crosses the river in less than half a mile. The take-out is a rough boat ramp on the north side of the river.

The Avery Ranger Station is 16.5 miles upstream from Calder. Turn right off the St. Joe River Road, then take an immediate left to a bridge across the river. The put-in is a steep and obvious trail just downstream from the bridge, on the north side of the river.

Boaters who want to shorten the trip will find good river access at the Huckleberry Campground, about 4 miles upstream from Calder.

A fourth access is about 9 miles upstream from Calder. Drivers headed east should watch for a dirt road about a half mile past Marble Creek, just before the St. Joe River Road crosses the river. The river is about 200 feet down this rough road.

PADDLE ROUTE

Flow information	• USGS Water Resources in Sandpoint
River gauge	• 12414500 at Calder
Historic flows	• Average 2,324; maximum 40,000; minimum 100

Most of the whitewater in this trip is between the ranger station and Marble Creek. Indeed, the upper stretch can be far too violent in spring for all but the most experienced boaters. Rapids are more scattered between Marble Creek and Huckleberry Campground, and are nearly nonexistent between the campground and Calder. The river is too low for canoeing when flows drop below 750 cfs, usually by August.

Among the common wildlife are ospreys and deer. Moose are less common. Houses and cabins, plus a few restaurants, are scattered along the shoreline.

Boaters who want to experience more of the river will find many other accesses in the 33 miles between Calder and Lake Coeur d'Alene.

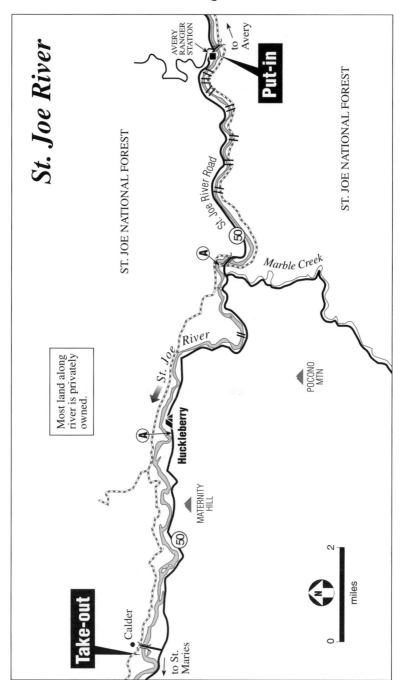

Powerboats may be encountered anywhere downstream from the town of St. Joe, and become common near St. Maries. The final 5-mile stretch is especially lovely (see trip 39).

The farther upstream one heads from the Avery Ranger Station, the more severe the whitewater and the fewer the opportunities for safe paddling. Rapids in Skookum Canyon, a narrow chasm between Packsaddle and Turner Flat Campgrounds, range to a dangerous Class 4 rating. Tumble Down Falls, near the Conrad Crossing Campground, is a 6-foot drop preceded by several hundred yards of violent rapids.

Wilderness adventurers enjoy a short season on the 17 roadless miles of the St. Joe between Heller Creek and the Spruce Tree Campground. Here, the whitewater ranges to a remote and potentially deadly Class 5. Logjams are common. This is a paradise for hikers, but a hellish place for paddlers who do not have the experience or equipment for extreme conditions.

41 • St. Maries River

Distance	•	7 miles
Time	•	2–3 hours
Season	•	March through November
Shuttle	•	7 miles, pavement, gravel, dirt
Rating	•	Class 1
Hazards	•	Strainers, deadheads
Information	•	St. Maries Ranger Station in St. Maries
Maps	•	USGS St. Maries, plus St. Joe National Forest map

North Idaho has no shortage of great boating water. The Selway, Salmon, Snake, and Moyie are revered by whitewater junkies everywhere. Canoeists ply the St. Joe, Priest, Coeur d'Alene, and Pack Rivers. Powerboats cut V's in the region's three large lakes.

With so much competition, it's no wonder the lower portion of the St. Maries River is often overlooked. The river begins in the Grandmother Mountain area southeast of Clarkia, Idaho, and runs 44 miles before it empties into the St. Joe River at the town of St. Maries. Sluggish and broad in its final miles, the lower river has nothing to offer whitewater enthusiasts. Anglers can find better luck elsewhere. And while some powerboaters use the river, most prefer to stick to the larger

Autumn on lower St. Maries River (Rich Landers photo)

St. Joe or nearby Lake Coeur d'Alene rather than risk bashing their boats against the deadheads that rise slightly above the surface or lurk just beneath it.

All the better for canoeists and kayakers, for whom the St. Maries offers a lazy drift through scenic forests and wetlands. Cedar trees shade the shoreline, sharing space with cottonwoods, aspen, and a variety of shrubs that offer brilliant displays in mid-October. The surrounding hills are evergreen forests dotted with Western larch that turn yellow in fall. Waterfowl viewing is prime in the spring, while rope swings tempt visitors in summer.

ACCESS

To reach the put-in from State Highway 3 (College Street) in the town of St. Maries, Idaho, drive south on First Street (behind the IGA

store). Two miles from the highway, the road turns from pavement to gravel and gets progressively rougher. Drivers should keep track of railroad crossings. The put-in is nearly 6 miles from the highway, just past the fourth crossing. A very rough trail leads over the tracks to the river. Boaters driving anything but a high-clearance vehicle should avoid crossing the tracks and park in the turn-out on the opposite side of the road.

The take-out is the St. Maries River Sportsman Access, a mile south of the town of St. Maries, on State Highway 3.

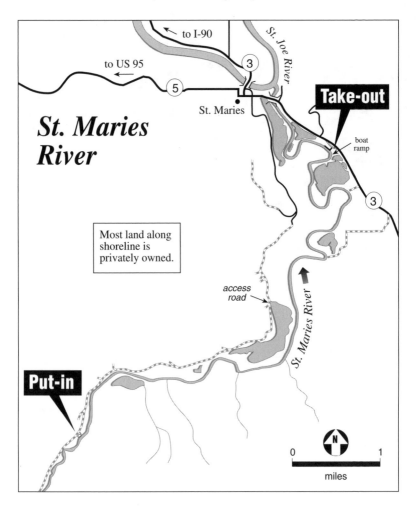

PADDLE ROUTE

Flow information • USGS Water Resources in Sandpoint
River gauge • 12414900 near Santa, Idaho
Historic flows • Average 338; maximum 9,120;
minimum 25

High banks keep most of the scattered development hidden from view, but they also hide the herons hunting in the wetlands that line this meandering river. The steep banks limit options for a mid-trip break since there are few places to beach a canoe. Most of the forests in the background are within the St. Joe National Forest, most of the shoreline is privately owned.

Although this portion of the St. Maries is generally placid, it has moments of rebellion. The evidence includes the debris hanging from cedar branches well above paddlers' heads. U.S. Geological Survey records show that flows peaked in 1995 during a rain-on-snow event on February 20 with flows reaching 4,450 cubic feet per second. On March 10, the river was running at 1,600 cfs. On May 23, it had dropped to 263 cfs. By August 31 the flow had dwindled to a still floatable 55 cfs. Get the drift?

42 • Selway River

Distance • 7 miles
Time • 3 hours or overnight
Season • Generally mid-June through July
Shuttle • 7 miles, gravel
Rating • Class 2, with one Class 2-plus stretch
Hazards • Numerous rapids
Information • Selway Ranger Station in Kooskia
Maps • USGS Goddard Point, Stillman Point, Selway
Falls, plus Nez Perce National Forest map

From its sources, reaching an elevation of 9,000 feet, and for most of its 90-mile journey, the Selway River flows through one of the largest roadless tracts of land in the lower 48 states, the Selway-Bitterroot Wilderness. The river becomes visible to roads and civilization fewer than 20 miles from its confluence with the bigger whitewater on the Lochsa River. In that short, final stretch, the Selway has enough

challenging whitewater and deep, green pools to keep a paddler busy for a weekend, and grinning through the week beyond.

The lower river flows through a narrow canyon, heavily wooded with Douglas-fir, spruce, and pine. Impressive cedars crowd its banks.

ACCESS

To reach the Selway, follow U.S. Highway 12 southeast from Orofino, Idaho, through the towns of Kamiah and Kooskia. About 62 miles from Orofino, the highway comes to the village of Lowell, where the Selway and Lochsa join to form the Middle Fork of the Clearwater River.

From Lowell, Forest Service Road 223 follows the north bank of the Selway. At 7 miles, Road 661 takes off to the south, following O'Hara Creek. The beach where the two roads meet is an excellent take-out for a half day of boating.

Skirting whitewater above the put-in on Selway River
(Dan Hansen photo)

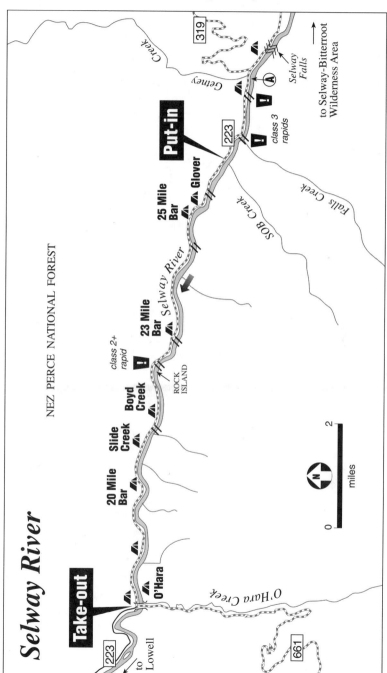

Selway River

NEZ PERCE NATIONAL FOREST

Take-out

223

to Lowell

O'Hara

O'Hara Creek

661

20 Mile Bar

Slide Creek

Boyd Creek

class 2+ rapid

ROCK ISLAND

23 Mile Bar

Selway River

25 Mile Bar

Glover

Put-in

223

SOB Creek

Falls Creek

Gedney Creek

319

Selway Falls

class 3 rapids

to Selway-Bitterroot Wilderness Area

N

0   miles   2

Road 223 turns from rough pavement to even rougher gravel at O'Hara Creek. Eleven miles upstream from O'Hara is Selway Falls, which should not be attempted in any manner of boat. Paddlers skilled in negotiating Class 3 whitewater (and with the proper equipment, including helmets) can launch at Getney Creek, just downstream from the falls. Two major rapids are in the next 1.5 miles.

The recommended put-in for intermediate paddlers is a small, unnamed turnout 2 miles downstream from Getney Creek.

PADDLE ROUTE

Flow information • USGS Water Resources in Sandpoint
River gauge • 13336500 near Lowell
Historic flows • Average 3,695; maximum 45,300; minimum 150

Between the put-in and O'Hara Creek, the river is studded with many rapids, interspersed with lovely pools and riffles. The toughest water, a challenging Class 2-plus, is a little more than halfway through the trip, where the river splits around Rock Island. Boaters should pick the left channel and scout the rapids from shore.

If 7 miles on the Selway isn't enough, paddlers can continue downstream. From the O'Hara take-out, it's another 7 miles to the confluence with the Lochsa. From there, paddlers can continue downstream about 6 miles on the Middle Fork of the Clearwater River to the town of Sylvanite. Both the lower Selway and the upper Clearwater are studded with whitewater, which should be scouted from the road and again from shore.

While the Selway is blessed with a plethora of Forest Service campgrounds, most are small and fill quickly. Those who travel light can load gear into a boat and take their pick of numerous gravel bars on the roadless south side of the river.

Lowell is headquarters for several rafting companies. Three Rivers Resort has a private campground, motel, and cabins, along with a small store and restaurant. The resort is a good source for up-to-date river information.

Because its headwaters are protected, the Selway has not suffered as much from logging as many other Idaho streams. It holds healthy numbers of native cutthroat trout. Special fishing regulations are enforced. Other regulations apply, and anglers are encouraged to gently release their catch.

OREGON

43 · Grande Ronde River
(Troy to Highway 129)

Distance	•	19 miles
Time	•	5 hours or overnight
Season	•	Generally March through November
Shuttle	•	17 miles, gravel
Rating	•	Class 2
Hazards	•	Strong eddies; tricky boulder-strewn stretches in low flows; rattlesnakes, poison oak
Information	•	Walla Walla Ranger Station in Walla Walla; Bureau of Land Management river rangers based at Minam
Maps	•	USGS Troy (Oregon), Saddle Butte (Washington), Mountain View (Washington), plus Umatilla National Forest map

The Grande Ronde River is fed by water from sources in the region's stunning and pristine backcountry, including the Elkhorn Mountains, the Eagle Cap Wilderness, and the Wenaha–Tucannon Wilderness. The river takes on its own character as it rumbles down from forests, through tortured canyonlands, under towering basalt cliffs, and to the breaks lined with sage and prickly pear cactus.

This trip features the most accessible and least dangerous section within 83 miles of popular floating from the confluence with the Wallowa River downstream to the confluence with the Snake River.

The area holds a wide range of notable wildlife, including elk, deer, bighorn sheep, raccoons, and otters, plus golden and bald eagles. Anglers can hook rainbow trout as well as steelhead in fall and early spring.

The Grande Ronde below and above the section featured in this trip involves roadless stretches, lengthy car shuttles, and Class 3 and Class 4 rapids. Above this stretch, the 44 miles of Grande Ronde downstream from Minam, Oregon, was designated "wild and scenic" by Congress in 1988. That stretch also includes Class 3 rapids and is a popular three-day trip for rafters. From Highway 129 to the confluence with the Snake are 18 miles of remote paddling, requiring a 4-hour shuttle. That trip includes Class 2 rapids and one Class 4 (with a difficult portage) at The Narrows, about 5 miles above the confluence.

The trip described here is within the limits of intermediate paddlers, with play spots that will appeal to advanced paddlers as well. This section is designated a "recreation river," which provides some restrictions on shoreline development. Private land is scattered within

Grande Ronde River near Troy (Rich Landers photo)

U.S. Bureau of Land Management and state land. Paddlers must stay off private land. Be warned that nothing pushes a rancher's hot button faster than the sight of a campfire in this arid landscape. The safest course is to stay below the high-water mark except in designated public access areas and campsites.

This route can be run as a day trip or a boat-camping trip. Stretches of flatwater are jazzed up with numerous Class 1–2 rapids. Scouting the rapids is easy, since roads parallel the river in this stretch. Car-camping also is possible, allowing boaters to travel light.

ACCESS

To reach the take-out from Asotin, Washington, drive south on State Highway 129 about 33 miles, through Anatone (no services), to the Grande Ronde River. Note that the last 10 miles from Field Springs State Park involve a slow, steep descent down the curvy Rattlesnake Grade. Cross the bridge over the river. The take-out is at the fishing access downstream of the bridge across from Boggan's Oasis Cafe.

To reach the put-in, go to the north side of the Highway 129 bridge and head west along the Grande Ronde River on Asotin County Road 100. Drive 17 dusty miles to Troy, Oregon. Take this opportunity to note several public access sites and primitive camping areas along the road. Troy offers food and camping, but no gas station. Drive through town, crossing the bridge over the Grande Ronde River. Turn left to the put-in at Varney Park.

Paddlers can add 7 miles of floating with an optional extension. In Troy, don't cross the bridge over the Grande Ronde River. Instead, bear right and cross the bridge over the Wenaha River. Then follow the county road paralleling the Grande Ronde upstream 7 miles to Wildcat Creek. The undeveloped access has a camping area nearby.

PADDLE ROUTE

Flow information	• National Weather Service in Portland
River gauge	• 13333000 at Troy
Historic flows	• Average 3,016; maximum 35,700; minimum 344

Ideal paddling conditions for canoeists in this stretch are roughly 2,000 to 3,000 cfs. At lower flows, exposed boulders can make paddling trickier. Higher flows wash out many of the riffles, but create powerful hydraulics and eddylines. The map in this book highlights rapids in the Class 1-plus to Class 2 range. But numerous splashy riffles occur between each notable rapid.

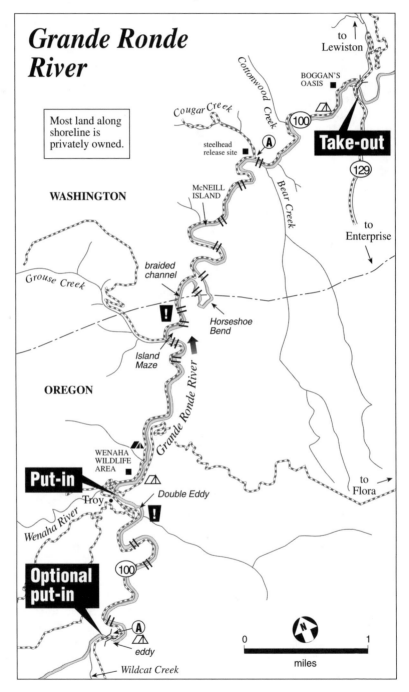

Grande Ronde River

to Lewiston

BOGGAN'S OASIS

Most land along shoreline is privately owned.

Cottonwood Creek

Cougar Creek

steelhead release site

(A)

Take-out

100

129

to Enterprise

WASHINGTON

McNEILL ISLAND

Bear Creek

braided channel

Grouse Creek

!

Horseshoe Bend

Island Maze

Grande Ronde River

OREGON

to Flora

WENAHA WILDLIFE AREA

Put-in

Troy

Double Eddy

!

Wenaha River

100

Optional put-in

(A)

eddy

N

0   1

miles

Wildcat Creek

The first hazard for canoeists starting at Wildcat Creek is Double Eddy, a tight Z-curve above Troy that causes strong eddies. The Forest Service rates this Class 3 in high spring flows. The main hazard downstream from Troy is Island Maze, which includes a braided channel and a sizable drop. In flows below 2,700 cfs, the only way to get through without pounding rocks is a channel at river-right. Stay river-right at McNeill Island, the only named island on the river.

Anglers who don't have fishing licenses for both Oregon and Washington should note that the river crosses state lines twice at Horseshoe Bend.

Although the Walla Walla Ranger District has information on this section, the BLM's Grande Ronde river rangers based at Minam may have a better handle on river conditions. Also check at Minam for details on the ever more restrictive rules for human waste and fire pans.

Shuttle services traditionally have been available from Boggan's Oasis. A helpful mile-by-mile river runner's map, "Wallowa and Grande Ronde Wild and Scenic Rivers," is available from the Walla Walla Ranger District.

MONTANA

44 • Clark Fork River

Distance	•	22.5 miles
Time	•	6–8 hours or overnight
Season	•	Virtually year-round
Shuttle	•	20 miles, pavement
Rating	•	Class 1, with some Class 2–3
Hazards	•	Bridge abutments, rocks, rapids
Information	•	Quinns Hot Springs Resort near Paradise
Maps	•	USGS St. Regis, Keystone Peak, Quinns Hot Springs, plus Lolo National Forest map

Although State Highway 135 parallels the river for most of this route, the Clark Fork River offers a surprisingly backwoods experience. This stretch of the river skirts through the Lolo National Forest and a puzzle of private landholdings scattered along the shoreline. The trip ends near a commercial hot springs resort.

The Clark Fork can become seriously swollen with snowmelt gathered in the 333 miles from its origin near Anaconda, Montana, to where it empties into Idaho's Lake Pend Oreille. Generally, with the notable exception of the gorge near Alberton, it offers easy paddling with numerous splashy waves and a few challenges. Most of the river traffic consists of rafts and drift boats with anglers casting for rainbow trout. The fishing is best in March and April before the normal runoff, and then again from late June through October. Two campgrounds and several camping areas are available. Forest Service Trail 223 parallels much of the south shore.

ACCESS

To reach the put-in, exit Interstate 90 at St. Regis, Montana, and drive north to the four-way stop at the junction with Mullan Trail Road. (Note: milepost mileage begins here.) Drive north on State Highway 135 about half a mile. Turn right to the St. Regis fishing access site.

Traveling to the take-out allows you to scout many of the river's features. Continue north on Highway 135. Just before milepost 11, pull over to see the first significant rapids. Halfway between mileposts 11 and 12, pass a primitive campground accessible from the road or the river. Other campsites on national forest land are found just downstream from this campground on river-left. Halfway between mileposts 12 and 13, pass the optional take-out at the developed Ferry Landing boat launch.

Just before milepost 16, pull over to scout Cascade Rapids (Class 3). Pass developed Cascade Campground another quarter mile downstream.

Bend downstream from Cascade Rapids on Clark Fork River
(Rich Landers photo)

An optional take-out on public land is at the big bend just past the campground. The recommended take-out is halfway between mileposts 19 and 20, across the highway from Quinns Hot Springs. However, this is private property: *permission must be secured* at the resort prior to the trip. The junction of highways 135 and 200 is 2 miles north of the resort.

PADDLE ROUTE

Flow information • USGS Water Resources in Helena
River gauge • 12354500 at St. Regis
Historic flows • Average 7,188; maximum 68,100; minimum 800

The river can be broad and featureless during high spring flows, but it moves quickly with power that must be respected. In summer, flows are mellow; rocks show in the riffles.

The first significant rapids follow a long straight stretch of slow water. The river bucks up against the rock rubble below the highway. Paddlers must pick their way through in low flows. Pass under a railroad trestle and note campsites on the bench between the river and the highway. The optional take-out at the Ferry Landing boat launch is on river-right just beyond the highway bridge.

Paddle downstream until small rapids on river-right warn that Class 3 Cascade Rapids are just ahead around the bend. In low water, paddlers can go to river-right before the bend and scout the rapids from the road. In higher water, stay on river-left to avoid being sucked into the rapids after rounding the bend. Eddy out on river-left and begin scouting or portaging where the railroad tracks depart from the riverbank. When flows are very high, say 20,500 cubic feet per second, paddlers without decked boats or adequate flotation can avoid the rapids by maneuvering through rocks along river-left. In typical summer flows, it is possible to sneak through Cascade Rapids without decked boats.

Note the optional take-out at the next big bend in the river. The area is marked by large rocks along the road and a small rocky peninsula that can become an island in high water.

Several waysides along the shuttle route help explain the great Ice Age floods that carved this valley and scoured the downstream landscape all the way to the Pacific Ocean. A short nature trail from Cascade Campground leads up to a good vantage of the Clark Fork Valley. The trail follows an old mine road that gave access to the area before the river road was built in 1934.

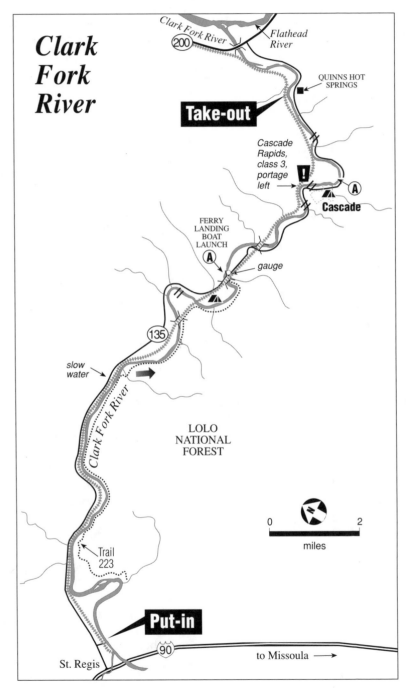

Clark Fork River

Clark Fork River

Flathead River

200

QUINNS HOT SPRINGS

Take-out

Cascade Rapids, class 3, portage left

!

Ⓐ

Cascade

FERRY LANDING BOAT LAUNCH

Ⓐ

gauge

135

slow water

Clark Fork River

LOLO NATIONAL FOREST

Trail 223

0   2

miles

Put-in

90

St. Regis

to Missoula →

45 · Flathead River

Distance • 54 miles
Time • 3 days
Season • Virtually year-round
Shuttle • 65 miles, pavement and gravel
Rating • Class 1
Hazards • Wind
Information • Confederated Salish and Kootenai Tribes at Pablo
Maps • USGS Buffalo Bridge, Round Butte, Melton Ranch, Sloan, Dixon, McDonald, Perma, plus Lake and Sanders County maps

Any whitewater paddler worth his neoprene is familiar with the three forks of the Flathead River. These famous whitewater streams tumble from the spine of the Rocky Mountains near Glacier National Park to feed the largest natural lake in the West.

Sandstone cliffs along Flathead River (Dan Hansen photo)

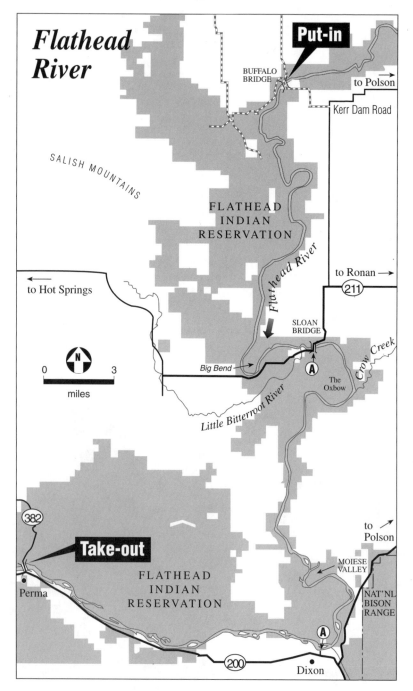

Flathead River

Put-in

BUFFALO BRIDGE

to Polson

Kerr Dam Road

SALISH MOUNTAINS

FLATHEAD INDIAN RESERVATION

Flathead River

to Ronan →

211

to Hot Springs

SLOAN BRIDGE

Big Bend

Ⓐ

The Oxbow

Crow Creek

0   3

N

miles

Little Bitterroot River

382

Take-out

FLATHEAD INDIAN RESERVATION

Perma

to Polson

MOIESE VALLEY

NAT'NL BISON RANGE

Ⓐ

200

Dixon

It is a gentler, though still impressive, river that leaves Flathead Lake and winds 70 miles through the sparsely populated Flathead Indian Reservation. The lower Flathead is broad, deep, and friendly. The surrounding hills are cloaked in juniper and bunchgrass, rather than the larch, aspen, and beargrass familiar to visitors to the three forks. In places, the river is hemmed by clay cliffs carved into spires, caves, and bridges.

Visitors to this remote country can expect to see golden and bald eagles, along with a variety of waterfowl and deer, elk, and the occasional moose. Those with sharp eyes or good binoculars may spot herds of grazing bison on the velvety hills of the National Bison Range. Lucky anglers hook toothy northern pike on spoons, 6-inch flies, or dead smelt drifted beneath bobbers.

The tribes prohibit boat motors larger than 15 horsepower. The quietest time to visit the Flathead is between March 15 and June 30, when all internal combustion engines are banned to protect nesting waterfowl. Typical flows range from an average of 7,430 cubic feet per second in August to an average of 19,710 cfs in June.

Permits are required for anyone who is not a Flathead tribal member. Fees are charged for boating and camping, and tribal fishing permits are required for anglers. Permits are available without advance notice at many restaurants and stores on and near the reservation, or at tribal headquarters in Pablo, Montana. Stang's Food Center in St. Regis, Montana, is the closest outlet to Spokane. Groups of twenty or more must get special permission from the tribes.

ACCESS

Road signs are rare in the reservation's backcountry, so reaching the put-in at Buffalo Bridge can be tricky. Drivers should keep a good map and compass handy. Virtually any road headed toward the river will eventually come to the put-in, though it may take many twists and turns in the process.

To reach Buffalo Bridge from U.S. Highway 93 in Polson, turn west onto Main Street, then take a right onto Seventh Avenue East. After 3 miles, turn right onto Kerr Dam Road, which is well marked. The road passes the Kerr Dam turn-off at about 3 miles. It makes a number of turns in the next 3 miles, before coming to an unmarked gravel road where drivers should turn right. Turn right again after driving a little more than a mile, and stay right where the road forms a Y. The bridge is about a half mile beyond the Y.

For three or four days of leisurely river travel, boaters should plan on ending their trip at the Perma bridge, 54 miles downstream from

Buffalo Bridge. Perma is 11 miles east of the junction of State Highways 135 and 200. The bridge is less than a mile north of Highway 200 on State Highway 382.

Alternative access points are Sloan Bridge, about 20 miles downstream from Buffalo Bridge, and the boat launch in Dixon, Montana, about 40 miles downstream from Buffalo Bridge.

To reach Sloan Bridge, drive west on State Highway 211 from Ronan, Montana. The paved highway turns sharply south at 10 miles and comes to the graffiti-covered bridge almost 3 miles past the bend.

Highway 200 is the main street for tiny Dixon. To reach the boat launch, drive about a quarter mile north from the highway on a gravel road opposite the U.S. Post Office.

PADDLE ROUTE

Flow information	•	Kerr Dam, or USGS Water Resources in Helena
River gauge	•	12388700 at Perma
Historic flows	•	Average 11,600; maximum 47,100; minimum 2,670

The four accesses mark rough divisions in the geography of the river valley. The most remote stretch and most of the clay cliffs are between Buffalo Bridge and Sloan Bridge. The river gorge broadens into a valley dotted with a few farms as one nears Dixon. At Dixon, the river turns west, and paddlers no longer view the Mission Mountains. The shore becomes more wooded downstream from Dixon, and anglers in powerboats are more common.

46 • Thompson River

Distance	•	30 miles with shorter options
Time	•	2 days
Season	•	Generally May through early June
Shuttle	•	26 miles, gravel
Rating	•	Class 2 above Little Thompson River, Class 2-plus below
Hazards	•	Fallen trees, shoreline brush; rapids; one cross-stream cable
Information	•	Plains Ranger Station
Maps	•	USGS Bend, Richards Peak, Calico Creek, Priscilla Peak, plus Lolo National Forest map

River rats seek big-water adventure on highly publicized Northwest rivers like the Rogue and the Salmon. The small-water adventure offered by the Thompson has its own set of challenges and thrills—without the crowds.

Solo on Thompson River (Tom Eggensperger photo)

The Thompson requires better-than-average paddling skills to maneuver through scattered rapids while avoiding the fallen trees that paddlers likely will find blocking their paths. After high water in spring 1997, the upper 18 miles of this trip were blocked in at least twelve places, each requiring a short portage. Getting caught in a strainer can be life-threatening, so a day on the Thompson requires extra attentiveness. Hawthorns with half-inch spines overhang the shoreline in many places, so a wide turn on this narrow river sometimes draws blood. Elsewhere, the river meanders through meadows, the current all but disappears, and paddling is not so much a challenge as a chore.

So why visit the Thompson? Because few streams are as lovely. The river begins at Thompson Lakes chain and runs 51 miles to its confluence with the Clark Fork River east of Thompson Falls, Montana. Streamside cottonwoods fill the air with their cotton-like seed pods. The many clearcuts one sees from roads are mostly invisible from the water. The roads themselves are hidden in the upper 18 miles of river, which is seldom paddled. Cabins sit streamside in places.

Wild roses bloom pink in June, complementing the Indian paintbrush and assorted other wildflowers that poke out of the thick underbrush. Paddlers have a good chance of seeing moose at close range. The Thompson holds good numbers of trout and threatened bull trout (actually a char), which must be carefully released.

ACCESS

To reach the river from Thompson Falls, Montana, drive east about 5 miles on State Highway 200. Turn north on the Thompson River Road (Forest Service Road 556) at milepost 56. The Forest Service road runs parallel to the river, as does a Plum Creek Timber Company road that usually is open to the public. The two roads sometimes are on opposite sides of the river; occasionally they are separated by only a few feet of brush, and sometimes they cross each other. Mileposts listed below are for the Plum Creek road.

(The river can be reached from Libby by driving southeast on U.S. Highway 2. The highway's junction with the Thompson River Road is 7 miles past the community of Happys Inn.)

For a long trip of flatwater and rapids, paddling can start near Bend Junction, just beyond milepost 31. Turn right onto the Forest Service road, and drive about a quarter mile to the river. Parking and an informal campsite are nearby.

The trip ends about 30 river miles downstream at Clark Memorial campground, on the west side of the river. The campground is about 5 miles from Highway 200, along the Forest Service road.

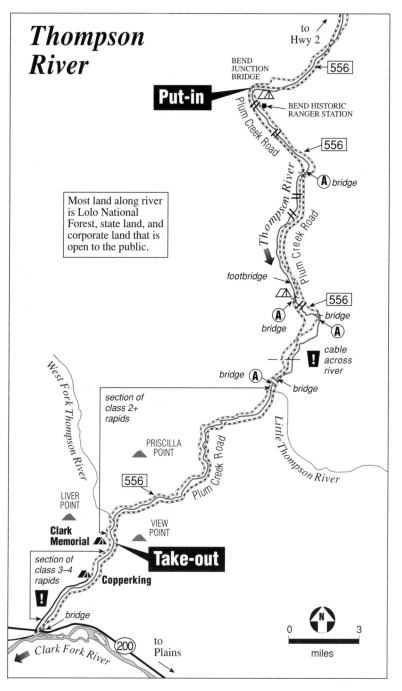

Thompson River

Most land along river is Lolo National Forest, state land, and corporate land that is open to the public.

to Hwy 2

556

BEND JUNCTION BRIDGE

Put-in

BEND HISTORIC RANGER STATION

Plum Creek Road

556

Thompson River

(A) bridge

Plum Creek Road

556

footbridge

(A) bridge

(A) bridge

(A)

cable across river

bridge **(A)**

bridge

West Fork Thompson River

section of class 2+ rapids

PRISCILLA POINT

556

Plum Creek Road

Little Thompson River

LIVER POINT

Clark Memorial

VIEW POINT

Take-out

section of class 3–4 rapids

Copperking

bridge

N

0   3

miles

Clark Fork River

200

to Plains

Four accesses are between the put-in and take-out, giving paddlers options to create trips to fit their skills and time restraints:

- The first access downstream from Bend is a bridge near milepost 27. The second is a bridge and campsite near milepost 21.
- To reach the third access, turn right (east) near milepost 19 at a junction with the Forest Service road. Drive about 1.5 miles to a bridge and meadow.
- The fourth access is a bridge near milepost 17, where the Little Thompson River flows into the Thompson.

PADDLE ROUTE

Flow information • USGS Water Resources in Helena
River gauge • 12389500 near the mouth
Historic flows • Average 445; maximum 5,360; minimum 67

While rapids are scattered through the trip, the final 12 miles from the Little Thompson River to Clark Memorial campground has the biggest and most frequent whitewater. This section is the least likely to be blocked by trees. Popular with local kayakers, rafters, and whitewater canoeists, this stretch can be scouted by driving roads along both banks. Intermediate paddlers can run it with proper equipment and skilled companions.

Below the take-out are rapids that should be attempted only by skilled whitewater paddlers. At one point, the river drops over a ledge just as it twists through a slot that can become clogged with logs.

Flows of about 1,200 cubic feet per second—higher than the river achieves some years—are ideal for the upper 18 miles of river. Higher flows increase the risk of getting caught in a strainer. The final 12 miles can be run with flows as low as 750 cfs.

While the entire 30 miles could be run in a single day, it would be a long one, with little time for fishing or other fun. Allow about 2 hours of steady paddling between the put-in and first access, and another 2 hours to the bridge at milepost 21. The next two segments require about an hour each. The whitewater section below the Little Thompson River takes about 2.5 hours.

An inch-thick cable strung across the river about 2 miles above the Little Thompson River can catch inattentive boaters by the neck.

Camping is at the Clark Memorial and nearby Copperking Campgrounds, or at informal campsites along the river. More campsites are at the river source at the Thompson Lakes Chain.

47 · Bull River

Distance	•	14 miles
Time	•	5 hours
Season	•	Virtually year-round
Shuttle	•	11.5 miles, pavement
Rating	•	Class 1 upstream from Bull River Ranger Station; Class 2 downstream
Hazards	•	Bridge abutments; whitewater; strainers
Information	•	Cabinet Ranger Station near Trout Creek
Maps	•	USGS Smead's Bench, Ibex Peak, plus Kootenai National Forest map

The Bull River offers a quiet float in view of Montana's snow-topped Cabinet Mountains, from which the river finds its source. Paddlers who carry binoculars may spot bighorn sheep on either side of the river valley. A lucky few startle moose and otters.

Horse crossing on Bull River (Dan Hansen photo)

The trip starts in a soggy meadow dotted with cottonwood trees and beaver ponds. The meadows gradually melt into forests toward the take-out. While the scenery is wonderful, this is not a wilderness trip. Cars on Highway 56 are frequently within earshot, and the two-lane highway is visible in places. Most of the land in sight is federally owned, and managed by the Kootenai National Forest. But the valley floor itself is mostly private, and dotted with houses. Livestock has overgrazed the riverbank in places.

ACCESS

Because much of this area is private land, access is limited. The trip has three access points, all on State Highway 56. The highway follows the river north from State Highway 200, about 5 miles west of Noxon. All road miles refer to distance from the intersection of the two highways. Access points are not marked, nor particularly obvious. Be sure to check your odometer at the intersection.

The most popular take-out is a wide gravel shoulder 2.5 miles up Highway 56. The site is identified by a large eddy and old wooden bridge abutments upstream, although the bridge itself is gone. The take-out is steep and rocky; footing is tricky. River-weary paddlers may be tempted to skid boats up the grassy slope a few feet from the rocks. Don't do it: This is private land! Take care to avoid blocking the landowner's driveway.

The most popular put-in is a small highway turnout 11.5 miles up Highway 56. If you come to the second bridge over the river, you've driven half a mile too far. A faint trail, often ankle-high with water in spring, leads to the put-in.

Between the take-out and the put-in is a third access, about 7 miles from Highway 200, where Highway 56 crosses the river.

PADDLE ROUTE

Flow information • USGS no longer monitors a gauge

The Bull runs 26 miles from its source at Bull Lake to the Clark Fork River at Cabinet Gorge Reservoir. From the uppermost put-in to the Highway 56 bridge, the river has scarcely a ripple. Oxbows and backwaters beg to be explored. Two private bridges and the highway bridge are the only hazards. Allow at least an hour and a half of steady paddling; two hours for a more enjoyable trip.

About 2 miles downstream from the highway bridge, just upstream from the East Fork of the Bull River, is a large meadow on the left. Administered by the Forest Service, the meadow is a good rest stop. Paddlers willing to hike a short distance can visit the Bull River Ranger

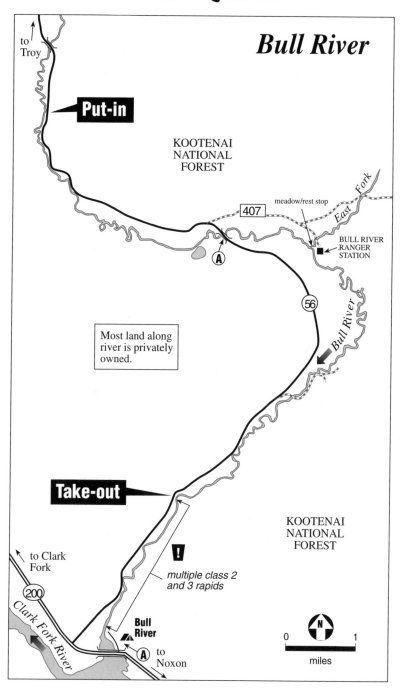

Bull River

Station, a 1909 structure that is no longer occupied but has become a state historic site.

The valley narrows and becomes more wooded downstream from its confluence with the East Fork. Downed trees are common, particularly on the outside corners of turns. A few rapids may rate Class 2, depending on river flows. Four private bridges cross the river. The stretch may be too rocky to paddle during low water.

The final 2.5 miles of the Bull River (below the final take-out described here) is much swifter than the upper sections, and has more obstacles and rapids that approach Class 3. It should be floated only by expert paddlers.

48 • Kootenai River
(Libby Dam to Libby)

Distance •	18 miles
Time •	4 hours
Season •	Year-round
Shuttle •	16 miles, pavement
Rating •	Class 1–2; one Class 2-plus rapid
Hazards •	Jennings Rapids; bridge abutments
Information •	Canoe Gulch Ranger Station near Libby
Maps •	USGS Alexander Mountain, Tony Peak, Swede Mountain, Vermiculite Mountain, Libby, plus Kootenai National Forest map

In a land of mountains, forests, and rivers, nothing stands more stark on the landscape than the concrete slab of Libby Dam. Towering like a skyscraper in the wilderness, the dam stilled 90 miles of the Kootenai River to form Lake Koocanusa. The reservoir (named for its connection to the *Koo*tenai, *Can*ada, and the *U.S.A.*) has its own fans in the anglers who troll for kokanee salmon and Kamloops rainbows, and the water-skiers who weave along its steep shores. Most paddlers prefer to start below the dam, where the river regains its current and its dignity, and begins its descent to Kootenai Falls, some 30 miles downstream from the dam.

This trip takes paddlers from the shadow of the dam to the town of Libby on a broad river with easy access and one notable rapid. (Note: A Montana record rainbow trout of more than 33 pounds was caught below Libby Dam in 1997.) Several shorter options include a leisurely 1-hour excursion that ends at a U.S. Army Corps of Engineers campground.

ACCESS

Paddlers covering the entire 18 miles should leave a car at the boat launch in Libby. Drive north on State Highway 37, which rises to cross the Burlington Northern Railroad tracks before spanning the river. Between the tracks and the river, turn left on West Thomas Road, which leads to a small city park and the boat launch.

To reach the put-in from Libby, cross to the north side of the Kootenai River on Highway 37, which follows the river upstream. After about 13 miles, just before the highway crosses the river, turn left onto Forest Service Road 228, which leads up the west side of the river. Follow this paved road 2.5 miles to the powerhouse turnoff and Alexander Creek Recreation Area boat launch.

Between the put-in and take-out are three accesses. First is the Corps of Engineers' Blackwell Flats Campground at the junction of

Kootenai River and Libby Dam (Dan Hansen photo)

Highway 37 and Road 228. Second is about a mile west of that junction, where a rough dirt road leads from the highway to the river's edge, opposite Canoe Gulch Ranger Station.

The third access is about halfway between Libby and Road 228, an obvious spot where the river is pinched to half its width between two constructed rock embankments. The Corps of Engineers, which operates Libby Dam, planned to build another dam here. Environmentalists beat back the proposal, which would have stilled Jennings Rapids and destroyed blue-ribbon trout water. The eddies on either side of the right embankment make good take-outs, easily visible from the highway.

PADDLE ROUTE

Flow information • Libby Dam recordings
Historic flows • Average 11,130; maximum 47,200; minimum 1,900

Paddlers who launch at Alexander Creek can explore inlets, coves, and heavily wooded Moonshine Island for a gentle 2.5 miles ending at Blackwell Flats. The campground has picnic tables, fire pits, and privies, but no drinking water. This makes a wonderful float for families, who may see bald eagles and a variety of waterfowl, as well as beavers, deer, and otters. Moose sometimes are spotted on islands near Blackwell Flats.

Downstream from Blackwell Flats, the river immediately narrows and quickens. Paddlers who are not cautious risk having their canoes wrapped around the Highway 37 bridge abutments by the swift current. Just below the bridge, the Fisher River joins from the south, leaving a muddy streak in the Kootenai during spring runoff. A mile below the bridge, paddlers hit Jennings Rapids, which can range to Class 2-plus during high water. The rapids can be portaged river-right.

Downstream from Canoe Gulch are a few mild rapids. The calm stretches grow ever longer and the shoreline more developed the closer one gets to Libby. In the 8 river miles between the abandoned dam embankments and Libby, paddlers are treated to distant views of Cabinet Mountain peaks. Powerboat traffic can be heavy here.

River flows, which are controlled by Libby Dam, typically remain high in summer to protect the eggs of Kootenai River sturgeon. The giant fish, among the oldest species on earth, was added to the Endangered Species list in 1994, when biologists estimated the population at fewer than 800.

Flows can range from 25,000 cubic feet per second in spring to 4,000 cfs in fall. Paddling is possible during all but the heaviest flow.

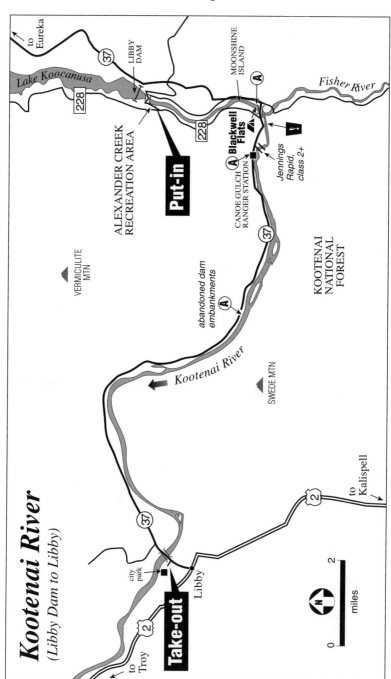

Kootenai River
(Libby Dam to Libby)

49 • Kootenai River
(Yaak River to Moyie River)

Distance	•	16 miles
Time	•	6 hours or overnight
Season	•	May through October
Shuttle	•	18 miles, pavement and gravel
Rating	•	Class 2
Hazards	•	Wind; scattered rapids
Information	•	Three Rivers Ranger Station in Troy
Maps	•	USGS Kilbrennen Lake, Leonia, Curley Creek, Moyie Springs, plus Kootenai National Forest map

For most of its length in the United States, the Kootenai River is within sight of roads. This trip, which starts in Montana and ends in Idaho,

Kootenai River near Idaho-Montana state line (Dan Hansen photo)

takes paddlers through a remote and heavily forested canyon, where cars cannot be heard or seen. An occasional house peeks over the horizon and trains screech and grind along riverside tracks, disrupting the solitude about every hour. Otherwise, river travelers likely will have the place to themselves.

Fishing is a big attraction, with healthy populations of pan-sized cutthroat and rainbow trout, along with a few lunkers. In early October, the shoreline becomes a mix of yellows and reds, with the deep green of pine forests in the background.

ACCESS

The trip starts at the Forest Service's Yaak River Campground, about 8 miles northwest of Troy, Montana. The campground has two entrances off U.S. Highway 2; boaters should use the one on the west side of the Yaak River, staying right at all turns in the campground until they come to a rough gravel road. The road leads about a half mile to the Kootenai River.

To reach the take-out, drive about 16 miles northwest from Yaak River Campground on Highway 2. At Evergreen School is a well-marked road to the privately owned Twin Rivers Campground. (Drivers who miss the turn will come to the Moyie River gorge a mile beyond.) The road to the campground twists downhill for 2 miles, turning from pavement to gravel halfway to the river. The owners charge for overnight parking, camping, and other activities. The campground is open May through October.

PADDLE ROUTE

Flow information • Libby Dam recording
Historic flows • Average 11,130; maximum 47,200; minimum 1,900

Broad and swift, the river is gentle for long stretches that are separated by rapids. The whitewater should not cause problems for intermediate paddlers. About 5 miles into the trip, the river crosses under an abandoned bridge at the old village of Leonia. Anglers should note the spot carefully, since it also marks the Idaho state line. Those with only Montana fishing licenses must reel in their lines.

About a mile beyond the bridge is a cedar-covered island with rapids at the head. There is a good, undeveloped campsite on a high bench at the tail of the island. A second island, 5 miles downstream from the first, also provides good camping. The islands and most of the south shore of the Kootenai is public land, administered by the

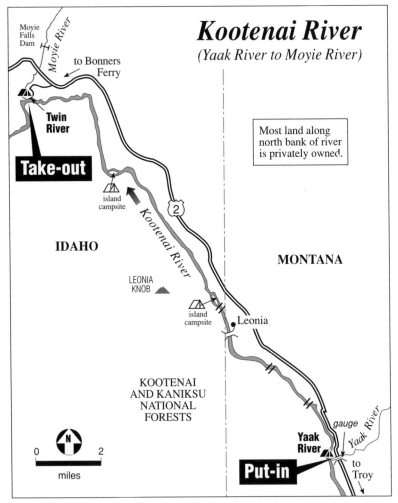

Kootenai River
(Yaak River to Moyie River)

Moyie Falls Dam

Moyie River

to Bonners Ferry

Twin River

Take-out

island campsite

2

IDAHO

Kootenai River

LEONIA KNOB

island campsite

•Leonia

KOOTENAI AND KANIKSU NATIONAL FORESTS

Most land along north bank of river is privately owned.

MONTANA

gauge

Yaak River

Yaak River

to Troy

Put-in

0 — 2

N

miles

U.S. Forest Service. The north shore is a mix of public and private land.

The Kootenai is controlled by Libby Dam (see trip 48), and flows can range as high as 25,000 cubic feet per second in spring and early summer to 4,000 cfs in fall. This trip is ideal when the river is at 10,000 cfs, give or take a few thousand. Campers should be cautious where they tie their boats and pitch their tents, since the river can rise several feet overnight, even if there is no change in the weather.

Strong headwinds can be a problem the last several miles.

50 · Yaak River

Distance	•	18 miles
Time	•	8 hours
Season	•	Generally May through June
Shuttle	•	16 miles, pavement
Rating	•	Class 2
Hazards	•	Strainers; whitewater
Information	•	Three Rivers Ranger Station in Troy
Maps	•	USGS Yaak, Clark Mountain, Mount Baldy, Newton Mountain, Sylvanite, plus Kootenai National Forest map

To whitewater paddlers, the Yaak River starts below Yaak Falls and runs just 10 miles through a scenic gorge. That portion of the river is one of northwestern Montana's whitewater hot spots, with rapids that rate

High water on Yaak River (Steve Thompson photo)

up to Class 4. Less famous are the miles of meandering river and mild rapids above the falls. Here, casual paddlers have time to cast a fly to the river's rainbows, cutthroats, brookies, and whitefish. They might spot a moose, and with the help of friends linking arms, hug ancient cedar trees.

The Yaak begins in Canada, crosses into Montana, and then flows 54 miles to the Kootenai River near Troy. This is timber country, with few services except the food, gas, grocery, and taverns at Yaak.

More than half the trip described here is through private land dotted with cabins and year-round homes. Some of the buildings near Yaak are historic. Elsewhere, the river flows through land managed by the U.S. Forest Service, with three public campgrounds. The entire route is paralleled by State Highway 508, which provides easy access.

ACCESS

To reach the put-in from Bonners Ferry, Idaho, drive east on U.S. Highway 2 along the Kootenai River. About 4 miles east of the Montana–Idaho state line, turn north on Route 508. It is 35 miles on this paved road to the town of Yaak, where the put-in is behind the Yaak River Tavern. The bar's owners have not minded boaters walking across the lawn to the river. As a courtesy, ask permission first. (Yaak also can be reached from Libby, Montana, by driving north 37 miles on Route 567. The paved road is narrow, steep, and curvy.)

Other access points are Pete Creek Campground and Whitetail Campground, at 3 and 6 miles downstream from Yaak along Route 508.

The take-out is 16 miles south of Yaak at Burnt Creek Road. The gravel road crosses the river less than a quarter mile east of Highway 508. The take-out is upstream of the bridge on the east shore.

PADDLE ROUTE

Flow information • USGS Water Resources in Helena
River gauge • 12304500 near U.S. Highway 2
Historic flows • Average 870; maximum 9,350; minimum 50

Starting at Yaak, paddlers enjoy about 2 miles of easy paddling on meandering, slowly flowing water. The river begins to narrow and gain speed about a mile upstream from Pete Creek. The first rapids are at the campground, which is out of sight from the river. From that point on, the river is punctuated with mild whitewater that can reach Class 2 in high flows. The final 9 miles from Hellroaring Creek to Burnt Creek

Road usually is too low for boating by early summer, when flows drop below 800 cubic feet per second.

Between Burnt Creek Road and Yaak Falls is 4 miles of whitewater that requires considerable skill. The falls itself must be portaged by all paddlers.

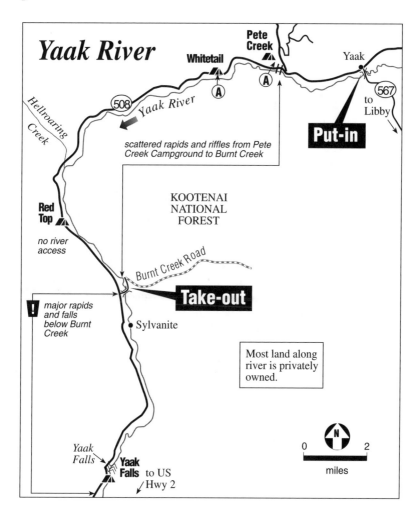

APPENDICES

APPENDIX A: Paddler's Equipment List

Paddlers should list the gear they might take on any trip. All of the gear might go on an extended trip; only part of it on daytrips. But always refer to the list when packing. Following is a sample list that can be personalized.

A signaling whistle should always be attached to life vests. In backcountry situations, put survival items (sealed in zippered plastic bags) in a fanny pack. Wear it at all times so the matches, knife, firestarter, etc., stay with you should your boat capsize and be lost.

BOAT

Paddles	Bail buckets
Extra paddle	Sponge
Life vests	Cushions
Grab lines	Extra dry bags
Lashing cord	Rescue throw rope
Flotation	

CLOTHING

Pile jacket	Underwear
Pile sweater	Long underwear
Long-sleeved shirt	Shorts
T-shirt	Long pants
Socks	Windbreaker

Rain gear
Gloves
Brimmed hat for sun
Pile or wool hat for cold
Bandannas

Sandals or booties
Rubber boots
Dry shoes
Wet suit or dry suit

SHELTER

Tarp
Tent and ground cloth
Tent stakes

Sleeping bag and liner
Sleeping pad

FOOD PREPARATION

Stove and fuel
Water bag
Water purifier
Pliers (for handling pots)
Pots, pans
Plastic cup and bowl
Spoon, fork
Large knife
Foil

Pot scrubber
Peanut butter
Hot drinks
Cold drinks
Snacks
Breakfasts
Lunches
Dinners
Salt, pepper, sugar, spices

PERSONAL

Toilet paper, wisely packaged
Biodegradable soap
Towel
Toothbrush
Floss

Candle
Lip salve
Hand lotion
Headnet

ESSENTIALS

Waterproof dump bag with
    complete clothes change
Plastic garbage bag
Waterproof bags and packs
Water bottles
First-aid kit
Signaling devices (whistle, mirror)
Map in waterproof case
Compass
Nylon cord
Knife

Insect repellent
Licenses and permits
Extra food
Flashlight, extra batteries,
    and bulb
Matches in waterproof container
Firestarter
Sunscreen
Sunglasses with straps
Repair kit for boat and other
    gear; include duct tape

ACCESSORIES

Notepad and pen
Reading material
Field guide to flowers, birds, trees, etc.
Zippered plastic bags
Camera and film
Folding saw
Grill

Plastic trowel (for latrines)
Latrine, if required
Fishing gear
Fillet knife
Collapsible bucket
Binoculars
Daypack
Pepper spray

APPENDIX B: Information Sources from Trip Summaries

The following sources are compiled from those mentioned in this book's fifty trip summaries. Use them as a quick telephone reference for specific trips. They are listed alphabetically according to the region in which the trip occurs.

BRITISH COLUMBIA

Creston Valley Wildlife Interpretive Centre, (250) 428-3259
Fernie Chamber of Commerce, (250) 423-6868
Kettle River Provincial Park near Rock Creek (summer only), (250) 446-2689
Lemon Creek Lodge south of Slocan, (250) 355-2403
Ministry of Environment, Lands, and Parks, West Kootenay District, in Nelson, (250) 825-3500
Ministry of Environment, Lands, and Parks in Penticton, (250) 825-3500
Summit Creek Campground near Creston, (250) 428-7441
Valhalla Provincial Park headquarters in Nelson, (250) 825-3500
Water Survey Canada in Cranbrook, (250) 426-4718
Water Survey Canada in Nelson, (250) 770-4451
Water Survey Canada in Penticton, (250) 770-4451
West Kootenay Power Company in Trail, (250) 368-0549
Wild Waves Sport Shop in Christina Lake, (250) 447-6561

IDAHO

Avery Ranger Station, (208) 245-4517
Bonners Ferry Ranger Station, (208) 267-5561
Bureau of Land Management in Coeur d'Alene, (208) 765-1531
Cabinet Gorge Dam, (208) 266-1531
Enaville Resort at Enaville, (208) 682-3453

Heyburn State Park near Chatcolet, (208) 686-1308
Idaho Fish and Game Department in Coeur d'Alene, (208) 769-1414
Old Mission State Park near Cataldo, (208) 682-3814
Pack River General Store northeast of Sandpoint, (208) 263-2409
Panhandle National Forests headquarters in Coeur d'Alene,
    (208) 799-5010
Priest Lake Chamber of Commerce, (208) 443-3191
Priest Lake Ranger Station near Nordman, (208) 443-2512
Priest Lake State Park near Coolin, (208) 443-2200
Sandpoint Chamber of Commerce, (208) 263-2161
Selway Ranger Station in Kooskia, (208) 926-4258
St. Maries Ranger Station, (208) 245-2531
Three Rivers Resort in Lowell, (208) 926-4430
Twin Rivers Campground northwest of Troy, (208) 267-5932
USGS Water Resources in Sandpoint, (208) 263-4123

MONTANA

Cabinet Ranger Station near Trout Creek, (406) 827-3534
Canoe Gulch Ranger Station near Libby, (406) 293-7773
Confederated Salish and Kootenai Tribes in Pablo, (406) 675-2700,
    ext. 595
Kerr Dam near Polson, (406) 883-4450
Kootenai National Forest headquarters in Libby, (406) 293-6211
Libby Dam recording, (406) 293-3421 or (406) 293-7751
Plains Ranger Station, (406) 826-3821
Quinns Hot Springs Resort near Paradise, (406) 826-3150
Three Rivers Ranger Station in Troy, (406) 295-4693
USGS Water Resources in Helena, (406) 441-1319

OREGON

Bureau of Land Management in Minam, (541) 437-5580
National Weather Service in Portland, (503) 261-9246
Walla Walla Ranger Station in Walla Walla, Washington,
    (509) 522-6290

WASHINGTON

Beaver Lodge Resort at Lake Gillette, (509) 684-5657
Boundary Dam Powerhouse north of Metaline, (509) 446-3083
Bureau of Land Mangement in Spokane, (509) 536-1200
Bureau of Reclamation in Ephrata, (509) 754-0215
Chelan County Public Utility District in Wenatchee,

(509) 665-7831, ext. 5
Coulee City Chamber of Commerce, (509) 632-5043
Fishtrap Lake Resort, (509) 235-2284
Forest Service Visitor Center in Winthrop, (509) 996-4000
Lake Roosevelt National Recreation Area in Kettle Falls,
    (509) 738-6266
Lake Wenatchee Ranger Station, (509) 763-3103, or 664-2704
    (toll-free from Wenatchee)
Lake Wenatchee State Park, (509) 763-3101; reservations,
    (800) 452-5687
Lyons Ferry State Park near Starbuck, (509) 646-3252
McNary Dam in Umatilla, Oregon, (541) 922-3211
National Resources Conservation Service in Colfax, (509) 397-4636
Potholes State Park near Othello, (509) 346-2759
Riverside State Park in Spokane, (509) 456-3964
River View Campground north of Yakima, (509) 952-6043
Soap Lake Chamber of Commerce, (509) 246-1821
Spokane County Sheriff marine deputies, (509) 456-2204
Sun Lakes State Park near Coulee City, (509) 632-5583
U.S. Fish and Wildlife Department in Othello, (509) 488-2668
USGS Water Resources in Pasco, (509) 547-2571
USGS Water Resources in Spokane, (509) 353-2633
Washington Fish and Wildlife Department in Ephrata,
    (509) 754-4624
Avista Utilities in Spokane, (509) 489-0500
Avista Utilities Post Falls Dam information recording,
    (509) 482-8043
Wenatchee Chamber of Commerce, (800) 572-7753
Wenatchee River County Park near Monitor, (509) 662-2525
Westbrook Resort north of Spokane, (509) 276-9221

APPENDIX C: Administration/Information Sources

NATIONAL FORESTS

IDAHO PANHANDLE NATIONAL FORESTS (HEADQUARTERS FOR
COEUR D'ALENE, KANIKSU, AND ST. JOE NATIONAL FORESTS)
3815 Schreiber Way, Coeur d'Alene, ID 83814, telephone
(208) 765-7223

Avery Ranger Station
H.C. Box 1, Avery, ID 83802
telephone (208) 245-4517

Bonners Ferry Ranger Station
Route 4, Box 4860, Bonners
Ferry, ID 83805
telephone (208) 267-5561

Coeur d'Alene River Ranger Station
2502 E. Sherman Avenue,
Coeur d'Alene, ID 83814
telephone (208) 769-3000

Priest Lake Ranger Station
HCR Box 207, Priest River, ID
83856
telephone (208) 443-2512

St. Maries Ranger Station
P.O. Box 407, St. Maries, ID
83861
telephone (208) 245-2531

COLVILLE NATIONAL FOREST
765 S. Main, Federal Building,
Colville, WA 99114
telephone (509) 684-3711

Colville Ranger Station
755 S. Main, Colville, WA
99114
telephone (509) 684-3711

Kettle Falls Ranger Station
255 W. 11th, Kettle Falls, WA
99114
telephone (509) 684-3711

Sullivan Lake Ranger Station
12641 Sullivan Lake Road,
Metaline Falls, WA 99153
telephone (509) 446-7500

KOOTENAI NATIONAL FOREST
506 U.S. Highway 2 West,
Libby, MT 59923
telephone (406) 293-6211

Libby/Fisher River Ranger Districts
Canoe Gulch Ranger Station
12557 Highway 37, Libby, MT
59923
telephone (406) 293-8861

Three Rivers Ranger District
Troy Ranger Station
1437 N. Highway 2, Troy, MT
59935
telephone (406) 295-4693

Cabinet Ranger Station
2693 Highway 200, Trout
Creek, MT 59874
telephone (406) 827-3533

NEZ PERCE NATIONAL FOREST
Route 2, Box 475,
Grangeville, ID 83530
telephone (208) 983-1950

Selway Ranger District
H.C. 75, Box 91, Kooskia, ID
83539
telephone (208) 926-4258

UMATILLA NATIONAL FOREST
2517 S.W. Hailey, Pendleton,
OR 97801
telephone (541) 278-3716

Walla Walla Ranger Station
1415 W. Rose Avenue,
Walla Walla, WA 99362
telephone (509) 522-6290

BRITISH COLUMBIA MINISTRY OF FORESTS

Cranbrook District
1902 Theatre Road, Cranbrook,
B.C. Z1C 4H4, Canada
telephone (250) 426-1700

Boundary District
P.O. Box 2650, Grand Forks,
B.C. V0H 1H0, Canada
telephone (250) 442-5411

Penticton District
102 Industrial Place, Penticton,
B.C. V2A 7C8, Canada
telephone (250) 490-2200

Kootenay Lake District
Ridgewood Road, RR 1, Nelson,
B.C. V1L 5P4, Canada
telephone (250) 825-1100

U.S. BUREAU OF LAND MANAGEMENT

Spokane District
1103 N. Fancher Road,
Spokane, WA 99212
telephone (509) 536-1200

Coeur d'Alene
1808 N. 3rd Street, Coeur
d'Alene, ID 83814
telephone (208) 765-1511

STATE AND PROVINCIAL PARKS

**Idaho State Parks and
Recreation**
5657 Warm Springs Avenue,
P.O. Box 83720, Boise, ID
83720-0065
telephone (208) 334-4199

**Washington State Parks and
Recreation Commission**
7150 Cleanwater Lane, P.O.
Box 42650, Olympia, WA
98504-2650
telephone (360) 902-8500

Riverside State Park
4427 N. Aubrey L. White
Parkway, Spokane, WA 99205
telephone (509) 456-3964

**British Columbia Ministry of
Environment, Lands and
Parks**
Parks and Outdoor Recreation
Division
Second Floor, 800 Johnson
Street, Victoria, B.C. V8V
1X4, Canada
telephone (604) 387-5002

**British Columbia Kootenay
District**
Box 118, Wasa, B.C. V0B 2K0,
Canada
telephone (250) 422-4200

British Columbia Kootenay District Area Office
Rural Route 3, Site 8, Comp. 5, Nelson, B.C. V1L 5P6, Canada
telephone (250) 825-3500

British Columbia Okanagan District
P.O. Box 399, Summerland, B.C. V0H 1Z0, Canada
telephone (250) 494-6500

FISH AND WILDLIFE AGENCIES

Washington Fish and Wildlife Department
600 Capitol Way N., Olympia, WA 98501-1091
telephone (360) 902-2200

Idaho Fish and Game Department
600 S. Walnut, P.O. Box 25, Boise, ID 83707
telephone (208) 334-3700

British Columbia Ministry of Environment, Lands and Parks
Fish and Wildlife Division
333 Victoria Street, Nelson, B.C. V1L 4K3, Canada
telephone (250) 354-6333

APPENDIX D: Sources for Maps

MAPS OF THE PACIFIC NORTHWEST

U.S. Geological Survey Earth Science/National Forest Information Center
904 W. Riverside, Room 135, Spokane, WA 99201
telephone (509) 368-3130

MAPS OF THE NORTHWEST AND CANADA

Northwest Map and Travel Book Center
525 W. Sprague Avenue, Spokane, WA 99204
telephone (509) 455-6981

TOPOGRAPHICAL MAPS ANYWHERE IN THE UNITED STATES

U.S. Geological Survey Map Sales
P.O. Box 25286, Denver, CO 80225
telephone (800) 435-7627

MAPS OF CANADA

Canada Map Office
615 Booth Street, Ottawa, Quebec K1A 0E9, Canada
telephone (613) 952-7000

British Columbia Ministry of Environment, Lands and Parks
Geographic B.C. Data Branch, Third Floor, 1802 Douglas,
Victoria, B.C. V8V 1X4, Canada
telephone (250) 387-1441

APPENDIX E: Paddling Groups

Borderline Boaters
1925 Highway 3, Christina
Lake, B.C. V0H 1E2, Canada

**Flathead Whitewater
Association**
P.O. Box 114, Whitefish, MT
59937

Flathead Paddlers Association
P.O. Box 7352, Kalispell, MT
59904

**Missoula Whitewater
Association**
P.O. Box 7893, Missoula, MT
59807

Spokane Canoe & Kayak Club
P.O. Box 819, Spokane, WA
99210

APPENDIX F: River and Lake Conservation Organizations

Rivers Council of Washington
1731 Westlake Avenue N.,
No. 202, Seattle WA
98109-3043
telephone (206) 283-4988

American Rivers
801 Pennsylvania Avenue,
Suite 400, Washington, D.C.
20003
telephone (202) 547-6900

**National Organization for
Rivers**
212 W. Cheyenne Mountain
Boulevard, Colorado
Springs, CO 80906
telephone (719) 579-8759

Idaho Rivers United
P.O. Box 633, Boise, ID 83701
telephone (208) 343-7481

APPENDIX G: Glossary of Selected Paddling Terms

Backpaddle To paddle backward to slow a canoe or to stop it.

Bail To remove water from a canoe with a bucket or sponge.

Bow The front end of a watercraft; opposite of stern.

Bowman The paddler in the bow of a tandem canoe.

Brace A paddle stroke used to stabilize a canoe. In a high brace, the grip hand is held high, the paddle at an angle in the water, the lower hand applying pressure against the water. In a low brace, the paddle is almost horizontal, the flat of the blade applying a downward pressure against the water.

Capsize To overturn.

Class A rating applied to a stream or section of current describing its navigability.

Confluence The point where two or more streams join.

Deadhead A piling or log, anchored below and afloat at the other end, lurking just above or just below the water surface.

Draw stroke A paddle stroke in which the flat of the blade is drawn directly toward the canoe to pull the craft to one side.

Drop A sudden pitch or unusually sharp dip in a section of rapids.

Dry suit Waterproof coveralls with snug-fitting collars for neck, arms, and ankles to prevent water from seeping in to soak insulating garments. For paddling in cold water.

Eddy Section of a current, downstream of an irregularity in the shore or a major obstruction, where the water flows upstream; often used as a rest stop.

Eddy out A 180-degree turn in direction from the main current into an eddy.

Eddyline The line between a swift downstream current and the circulating or upstream current within the eddy.

Even keel Properly trimmed to float in a level position; also describes spouse who isn't shaken by partner's poor paddling communication skills.

Falls Free-falling water over an obstruction. Heavy rapids also are called falls.

Ferry Angling the canoe so the current, striking the canoe's upstream side, drives the craft toward shore while paddling or backpaddling against the flow.

Flatwater Lake water or river section where no rapids exist. Sometimes a misnomer, since wind can create large waves on so-called flatwater.

Flotation Foam blocks or airbags used in canoes or kayaks to displace water and keep the boats afloat when capsized.

Forward stroke The basic or cruising stroke for propelling a canoe ahead.

Gauging station Streamside device that automatically measures water flow.

Grab line A rope at least 10 feet long attached to each end of a canoe for use in case of upset.

Gradient The average rate of drop in a river, generally expressed in feet per mile.

Gunwale (Also known as gunnel.) Strip along the top of a canoe's sides, extending from bow to stern, providing longitudinal rigidity.

Hull The main body of a canoe.

Hydraulics A term applied to the movements and forces of moving water.

Hypothermia The lowering of the body's inner core temperature as a result of exposure to cold water or air.

J stroke A stroke in which the paddle blade is thrust away from the canoe at the completion of a forward stroke, used to keep a canoe on course.

Keel Strip of molded or added material along the bottom center of a canoe, running from stem to stern, designed to reinforce the hull bottom and to minimize drift during lake paddling. A detriment in whitewater, since it interferes with maneuverability.

Lead canoe A trip leader's canoe, leading a group and selecting passages.

Lee Section of a waterway protected from the wind.

Lining Guiding a canoe downstream through rapids or shallows by means of a rope or line; opposite of tracking.

Peeling out Exiting from an eddy.

PFD Personal flotation device; a life vest.

Pivot To turn a canoe within its own length.

Poling Propelling a canoe, usually in a standing position, with a pole, either upstream or down.

Portage To carry a boat around a section of unnavigable water or between two sections of water.

Pry A paddle stroke that uses the gunwale as a fulcrum to thrust the canoe to one side.

Rapids Swiftly flowing water, tumbling among obstructions, creating considerable turbulence.

Riffles Swift, shallow water running over sand or gravel bottom, creating small waves. Could be termed gentle rapids.

River-left The left side of the river as you face downstream.

River-right The right side of the river as you face downstream.

Rock garden Navigable rock-strewn set of rapids requiring precise maneuvering.

Scout Examine a section of river or set of rapids to determine difficulty and best possible passage.

Slackwater Slowly flowing or still water without rapids.

Stern Rear section of a watercraft; opposite of bow.

Strainer Fallen tree or other debris with water flowing through it; potentially hazardous because it could hang up a canoe or swimmer.

Surfing In whitewater, riding the upstream side of a type of wave that breaks upstream. The hydraulics will hold or "surf" a boat in a stationary position while facing upstream. In flatwater paddling, riding downwind on the crests of large waves.

Swamp When a boat fills with water without capsizing.

Sweep boat The last canoe in a group, usually paddled by experts ready to assist those in front.

Sweep stroke A wide, shallow stroke, the blade barely submerged, used to pivot the canoe.

Thigh straps Straps attached to the side of the canoe and to the center of the bottom. When in use, they bind across a kneeling paddler's thighs, affording better control.

Throw line Length of rope used in rescue efforts.

Thwart Cross braces running from gunwale to gunwale.

Tongue A smooth V of swift water at the head of a drop or between two obstructions.

Track To paddle in a straight line.

Tracking Towing a canoe upstream with a rope; opposite of lining.

Trim The manner in which a canoe rides on the water: being level.

Tumblehome The inward curving of the sides of a canoe from a point at or slightly above the waterline to the gunwales.

Wet suit A close-fitting garment of foam sandwiched in nylon that provides insulation against cold water; allows water to seep in next to skin.

Whitewater A set of rapids.

INDEX

ABOUT THE AUTHORS

Rich Landers has been the Outdoors editor for *The Spokesman-Review* in Spokane since 1977. He has won conservation writing awards from the Idaho Conservation League, Washington Environmental Council, and National Audubon Society. Landers is the regional editor for *Field & Stream* magazine. His work has appeared in *Canoe & Kayak, Western Outdoors, Adventure Cyclist, American Forests, The Washington Post,* and other publications. Landers is co-author of *100 Hikes in the Inland Northwest.* His paddling experience extends from Baja to Alaska's Arctic National Wildlife Refuge, and from Maine to the estuaries of Puget Sound.

Dan Hansen is a fifth generation Washington resident. He grew up hiking and hunting in the Cascade foothills, and trolling for salmon in the San Juan Islands. Since 1987, he has worked in Spokane for *The Spokesman-Review* covering local government and various other subjects. His work also has appeared in *Canoe & Kayak.* In 1995, Dan and photographer Steve Thompson explored 420 miles of the Columbia River in a 13-foot inflatable boat with a 15-horsepower outboard motor to file a series of stories about life and recreation along the river.

Rich Landers (left) with his wife, Meredith, and daughters Hillary and Brook; Dan Hansen (kneeling) with his wife, Pam, and children Kelly and Kyle (Steve Thompson photo)

THE MOUNTAINEERS, founded in 1906, is a nonprofit outdoor activity and conservation club, whose mission is "to explore, study, preserve, and enjoy the natural beauty of the outdoors. . . . " Based in Seattle, Washington, the club is now the third-largest such organization in the United States, with 15,000 members and five branches throughout Washington State.

The Mountaineers sponsors both classes and year-round outdoor activities in the Pacific Northwest, which include hiking, mountain climbing, ski-touring, snowshoeing, bicycling, camping, kayaking and canoeing, nature study, sailing, and adventure travel. The club's conservation division supports environmental causes through educational activities, sponsoring legislation, and presenting informational programs. All club activities are led by skilled, experienced volunteers, who are dedicated to promoting safe and responsible enjoyment and preservation of the outdoors.

If you would like to participate in these organized outdoor activities or the club's programs, consider a membership in The Mountaineers. For information and an application, write or call The Mountaineers, Club Headquarters, 300 Third Avenue West, Seattle, Washington 98119; (206) 284-6310.

The Mountaineers Books, an active, nonprofit publishing program of the club, produces guidebooks, instructional texts, historical works, natural history guides, and works on environmental conservation. All books produced by The Mountaineers are aimed at fulfilling the club's mission.

Send or call for our catalog of more than 300 outdoor titles:

 The Mountaineers Books
1001 SW Klickitat Way, Suite 201
Seattle, WA 98134
1-800-553-4453
e-mail: mbooks@mountaineers.org
website: www.mountaineers.org

Other titles you may enjoy from The Mountaineers:

CANOE AND KAYAK ROUTES OF NORTHWEST OREGON, 2nd Edition, *Philip N. Jones*
The definitive flatwater paddling guide to northwest Oregon, including seventy outings for canoe and sea kayak enthusiasts.

AFOOT AND AFLOAT Series, *Marge & Ted Mueller*
The best-selling series of recreation guides for hikers, boaters, bicyclists, and car tourists, covering the entire Puget Sound and the San Juan Islands.

PADDLE ROUTES OF WESTERN WASHINGTON: 50 Flatwater Trips for Canoe and Kayak, *Verne Huser*
A flatwater paddling guide including information on location, distance, duration, shuttle details, best season, and more.

THE WATERFALL LOVER'S GUIDE TO THE PACIFIC NORTHWEST, 3rd Edition: Where to Find More Than 500 Scenic Waterfalls in Washington, Oregon, & Idaho, *Gregory A. Ploumb*
A five-star system rates waterfalls accessible to day hikers and Sunday drivers.

KIDS IN THE WILD: A Family Guide to Outdoor Recreation, *Cindy Ross & Todd Gladfelter*
A family-tested handbook of advice on sharing outdoor adventures with children of all ages and skill levels, including recommendations on equipment, food, safety, and family activities year-round.

BOATER'S SAFETY HANDBOOK, *American Outdoor Safety League*
Quick help for boaters and boat emergencies.

100 HIKES IN THE INLAND NORTHWEST, *Rich Landers, Ida Rowe Dolphin, and the Spokane Mountaineers*
The authoritative guide to the best hikes and backpacking trips throughout the Inland Northwest region of eastern Washington, northern Idaho, northeastern Oregon, and southeastern British Columbia.